THE GIANT BOOK OF CLASSICAL MUSIC

EASY PIANO

MW00799264

Produced by
Alfred Music
P.O. Box 10003
Van Nuys, CA 91410-0003
alfred.com

ISBN-10: 1-4706-1104-X

ISBN-13: 978-1-4706-1104-0

Piano keys: © Shutterstock / Ensuper, Brush stroke: © Shutterstock / foxie

Contents

by Composer

Contents

by Title

Air on the G String

(from Orchestral Suite No. 3)

Johann Sebastian Bach (1685–1750)
BWV 1068
Arranged by Jerry Ray

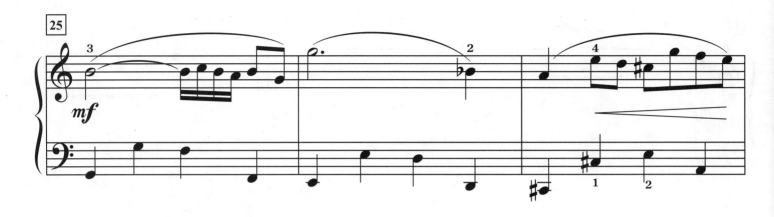

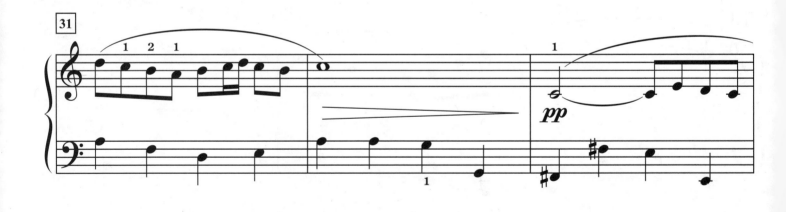

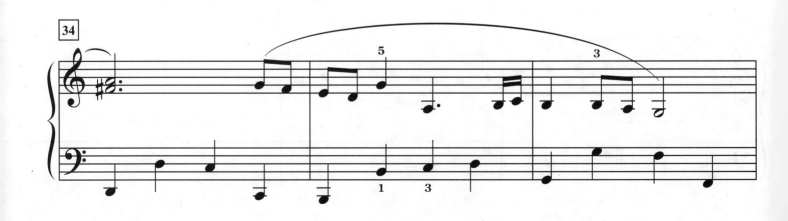

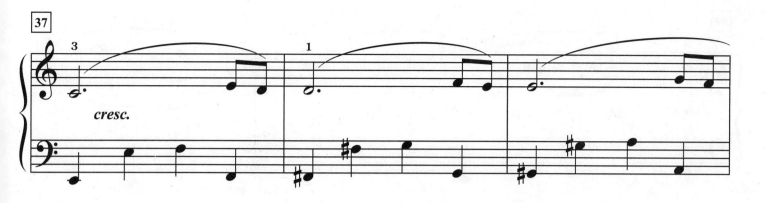

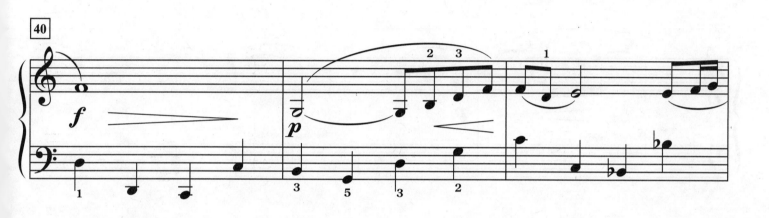

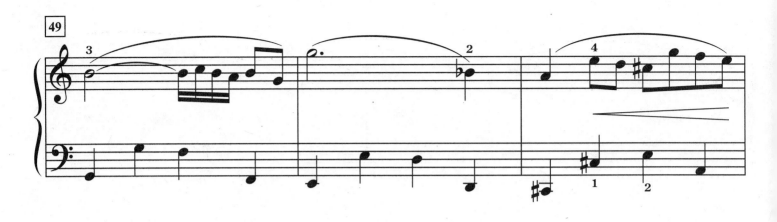

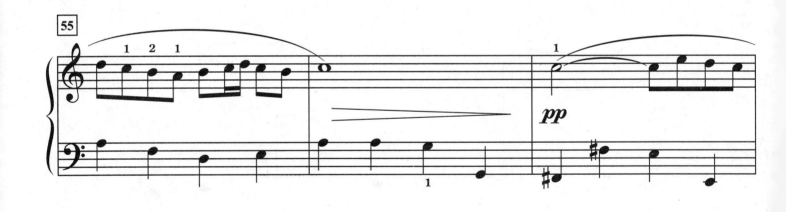

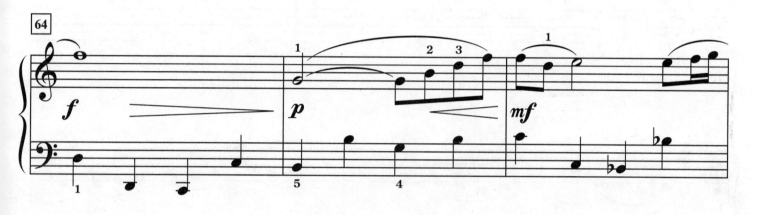

Brandenburg Concerto No. 3

(First Movement)

Johann Sebastian Bach (1685–1750)
BWV 1048
Arranged by Bruce Nelson

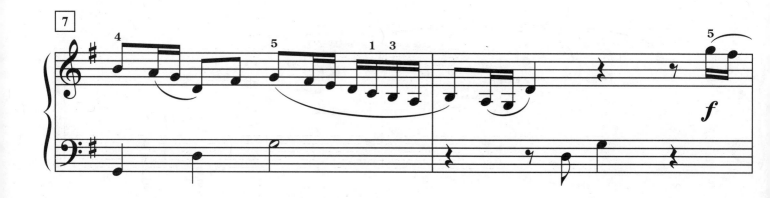

Prelude

(from Cello Suite No. 1)

Johann Sebastian Bach (1685–1750)
BWV 1007
Arranged by Bruce Nelson

Moderato

(pedal lightly)

simile

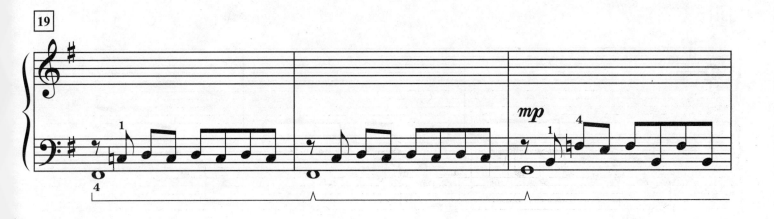

poco a poco cresc.

Freely

mf

Jesu, Joy of Man's Desiring

Johann Sebastian Bach (1685–1750)
BWV 147
Arranged by Bruce Nelson

Sheep May Safely Graze

Johann Sebastian Bach (1685–1750)
BWV 208
Arranged by Bruce Nelson

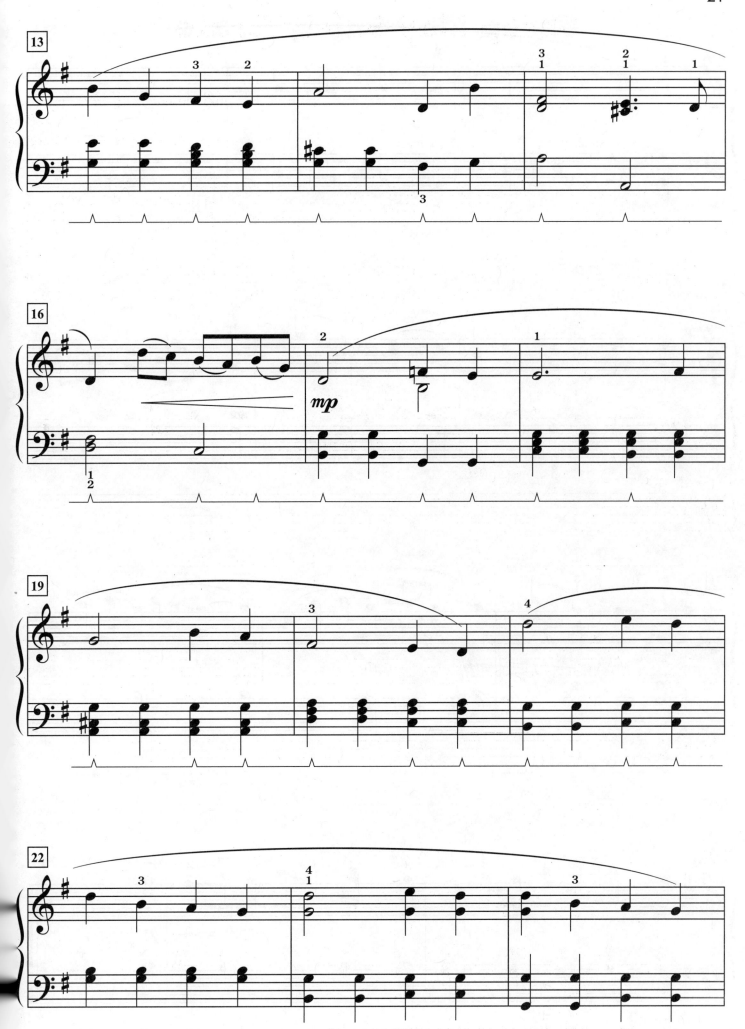

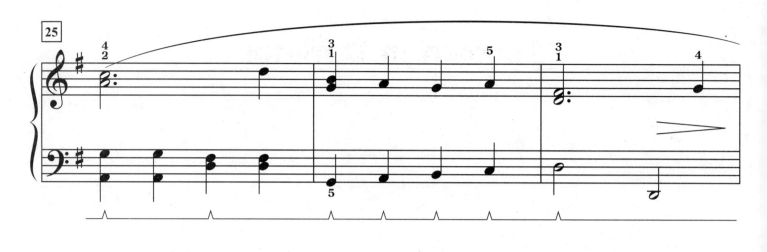

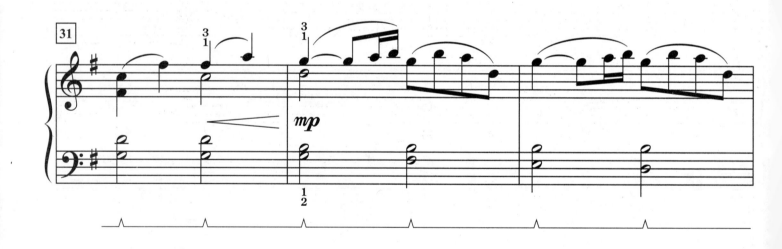

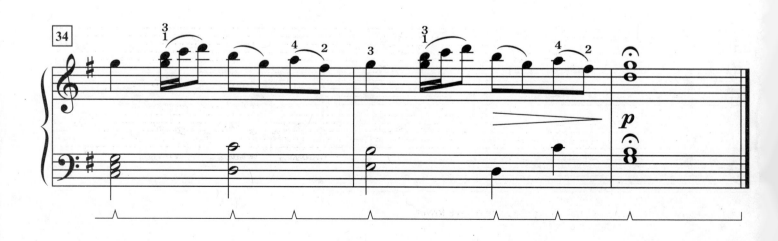

Toccata in D Minor

Johann Sebastian Bach (1685–1750)
BWV 565
Arranged by Bruce Nelson

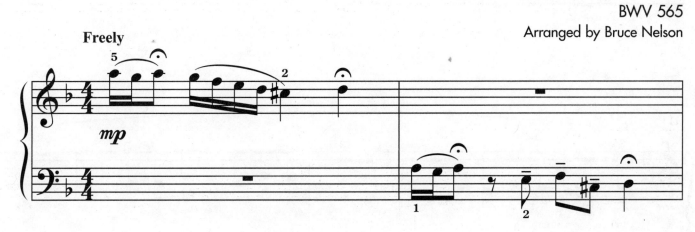

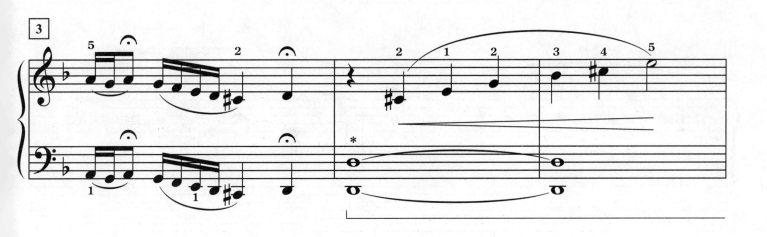

* The octaves in measures 4–7 may be played one octave lower.

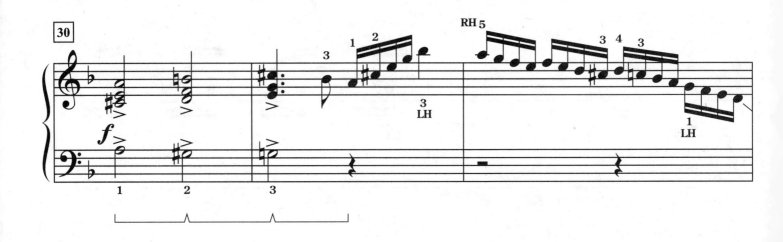

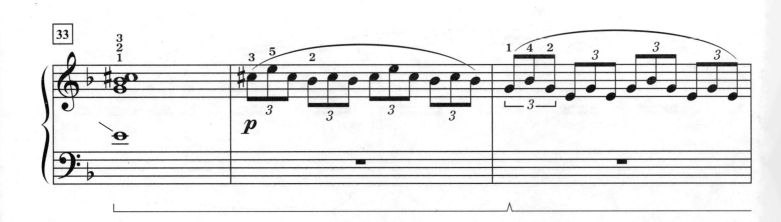

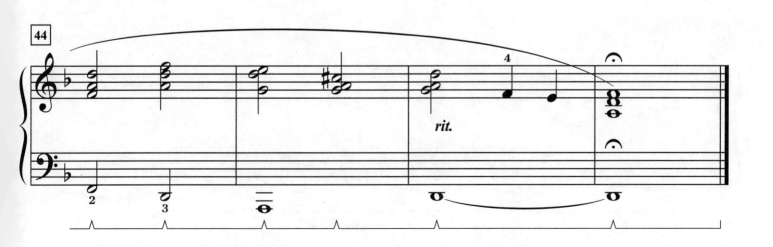

"Moonlight" Sonata

(Piano Sonata No. 14, First Movement)

Ludwig van Beethoven (1770–1827)
Op. 27, No. 2
Arranged by Mary K. Sallee

Adagio sostenuto

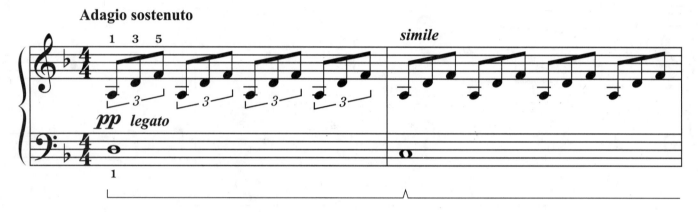

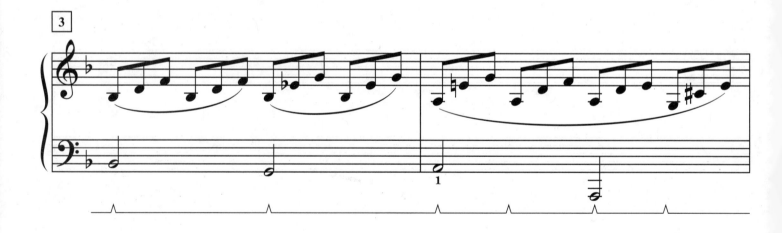

Ode to Joy

(from Symphony No. 9, Fourth Movement)

Ludwig van Beethoven (1770–1827)
Op. 125
Arranged by Mary K. Sallee

Allegro

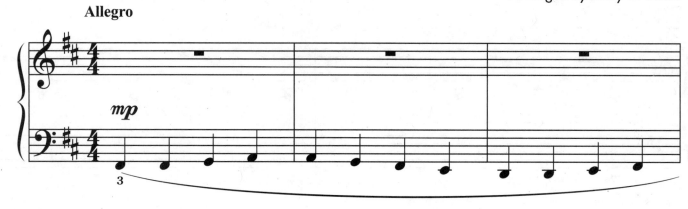

(a) The RH in m. 17 (and similarly in mm. 25–27, and 38) may be played:

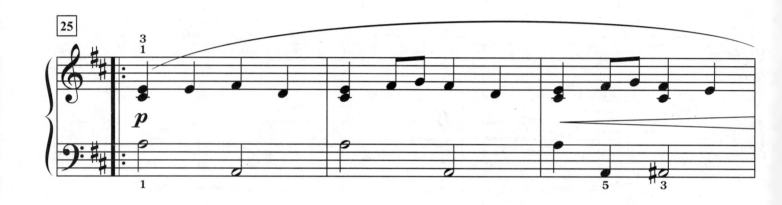

Egmont Overture

Ludwig van Beethoven (1770–1827)
Op. 84
Arranged by Jerry Ray

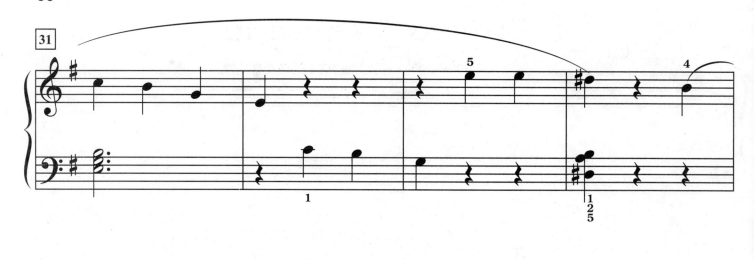

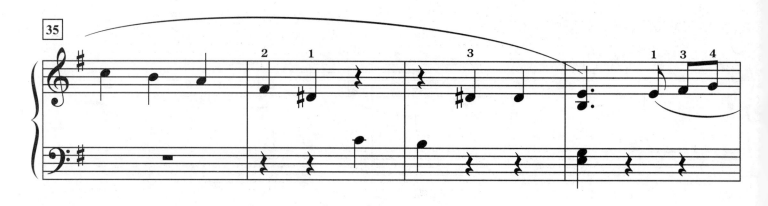

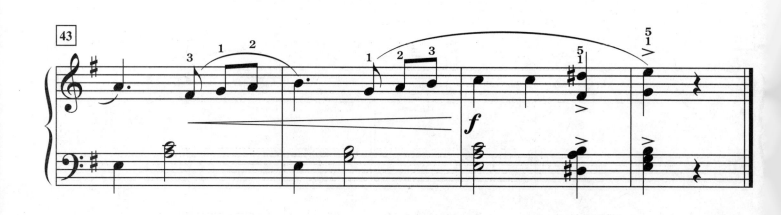

"Emperor" Concerto

(Piano Concerto No. 5, Second Movement)

Ludwig van Beethoven (1770–1827)
Op. 73
Arranged by Jerry Ray

"Pathétique" Sonata

(Piano Sonata No. 8, Second Movement)

Ludwig van Beethoven (1770–1827)
Op. 13
Arranged by Jerry Ray

Adagio cantabile

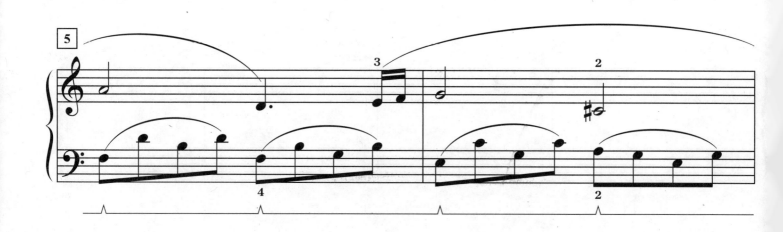

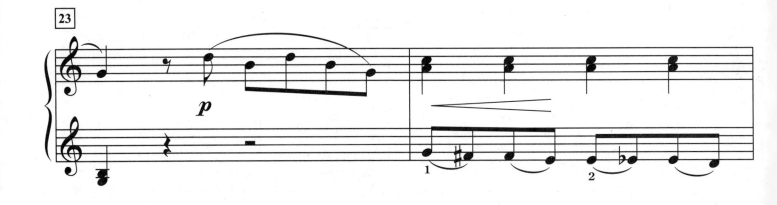

Symphony No. 5

(First Movement)

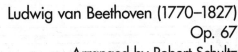

Ludwig van Beethoven (1770–1827)
Op. 67
Arranged by Robert Schultz

Allegro con brio

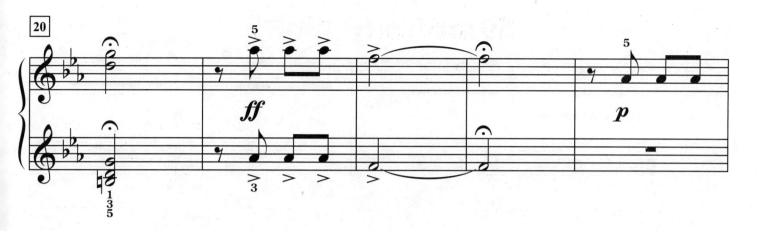

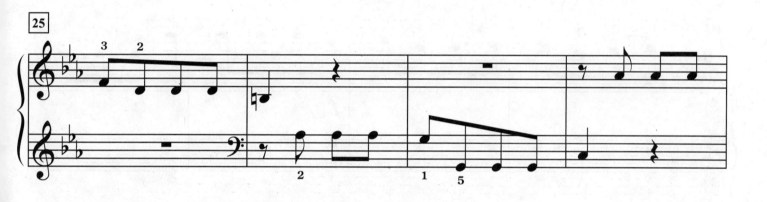

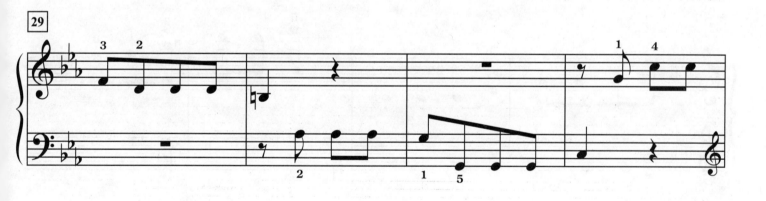

cresc. poco a poco

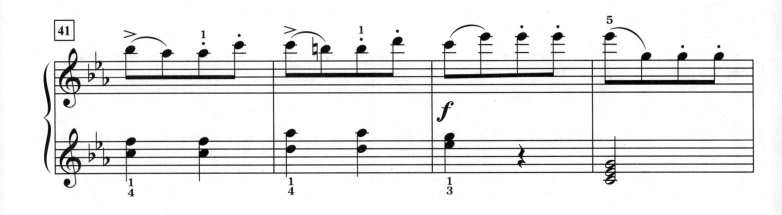

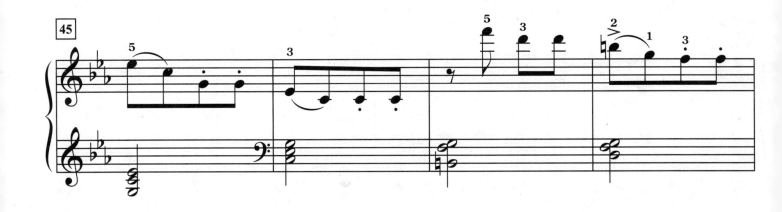

Turkish March

(from *The Ruins of Athens*)

Ludwig van Beethoven (1770–1827)
Op. 113
Arranged by Mary K. Sallee

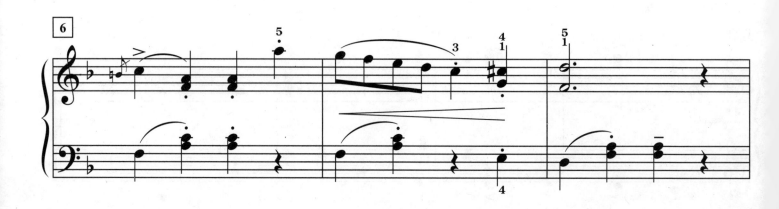

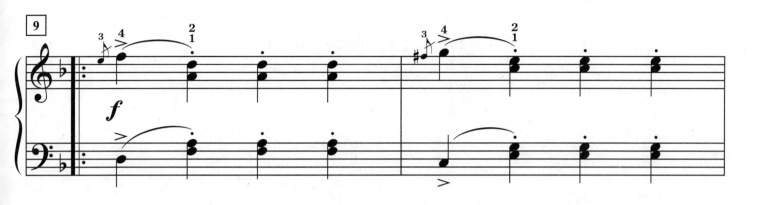

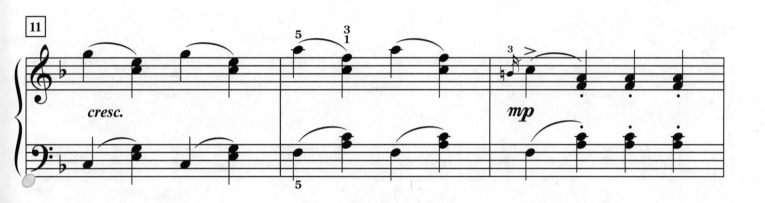

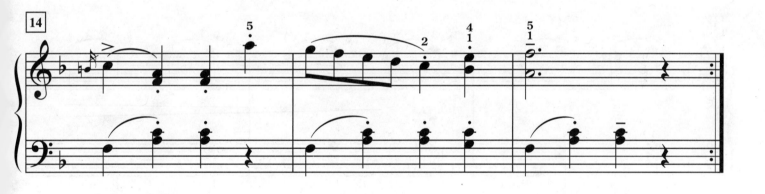

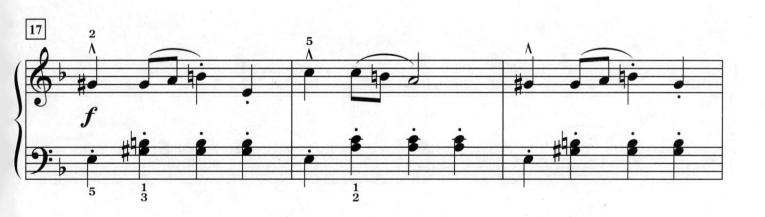

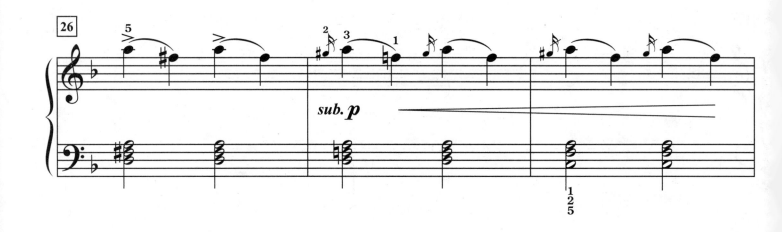

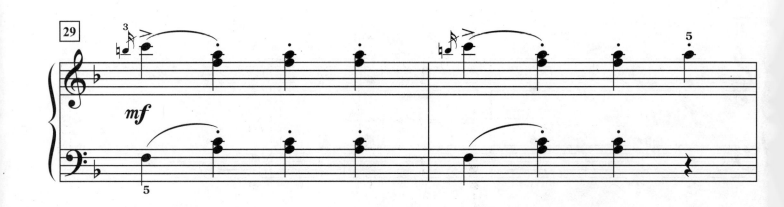

Habanera

(from *Carmen*)

Georges Bizet (1838–1875)
Arranged by Tom Gerou

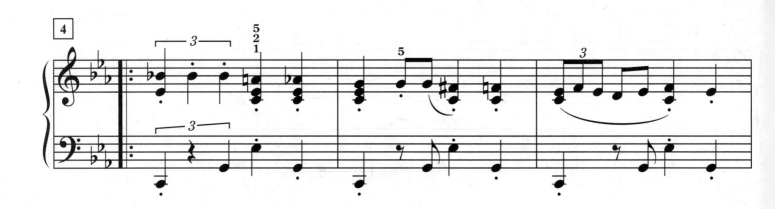

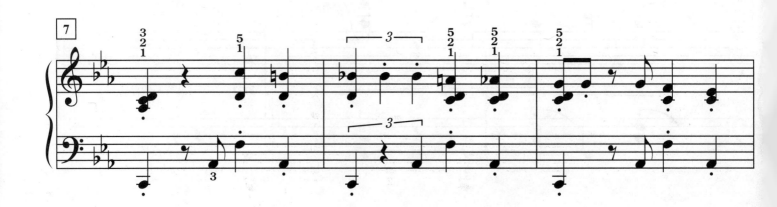

L'Arlésienne

(Prelude from Suite No. 1)

George Bizet (1838–1875)
Arranged by Robert Schultz

Allegro deciso

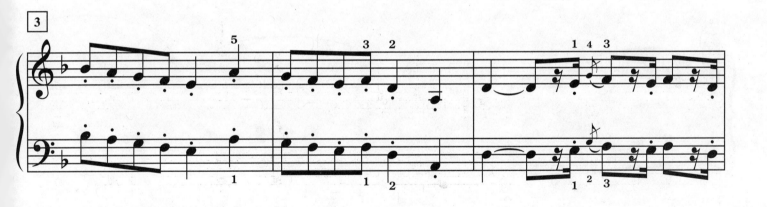

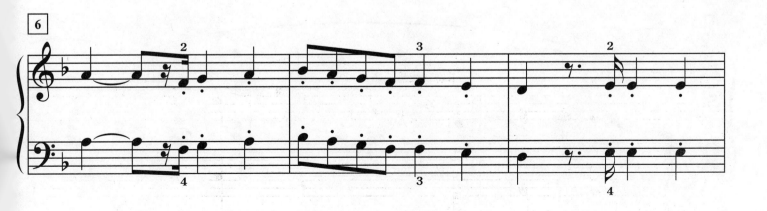

March of the Toreadors

(from *Carmen*)

Georges Bizet (1838–1875)
Arranged by Robert Schultz

Allegro giocoso

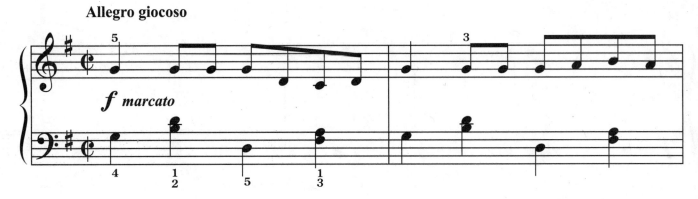

Toreador Song

(from *Carmen*)

Georges Bizet (1838–1875)
Arranged by Tom Gerou

Allegro moderato

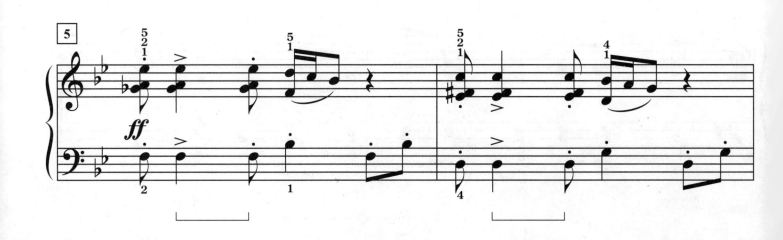

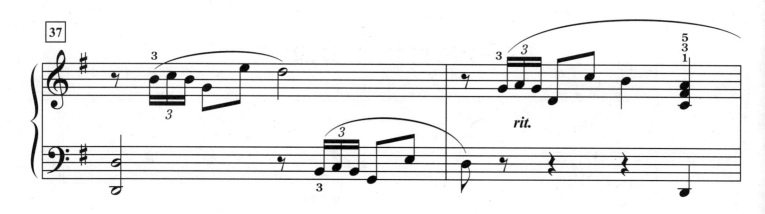

Polovetsian Dance

(from *Prince Igor*)

Alexander Borodin (1833–1887)
Arranged by Robert Schultz

Hungarian Dance No. 5

Johannes Brahms (1833–1897)
WoO 1
Arranged by Carol Matz

Waltz

Johannes Brahms (1833–1897)
Op. 39, No. 15
Arranged by Carol Matz

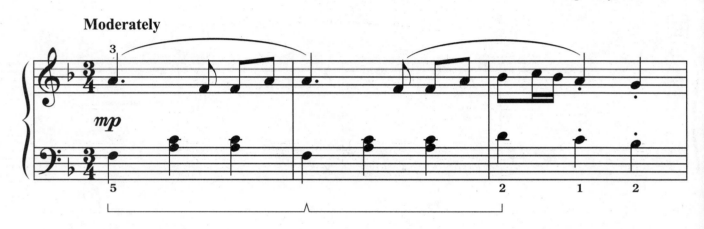

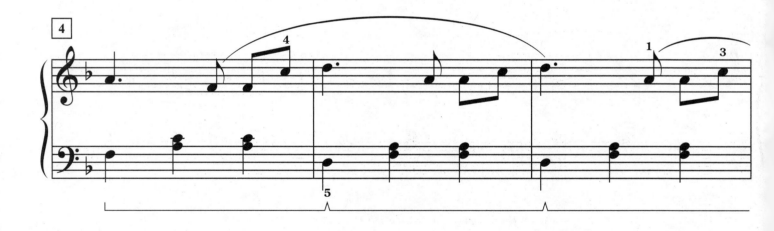

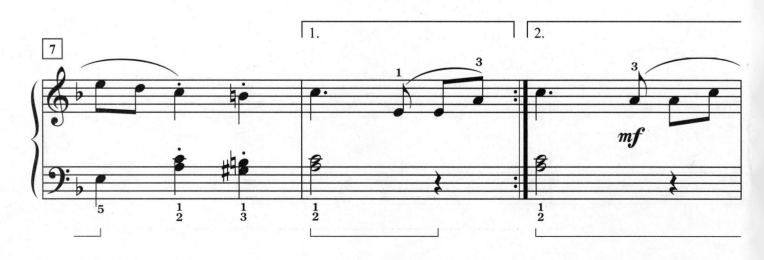

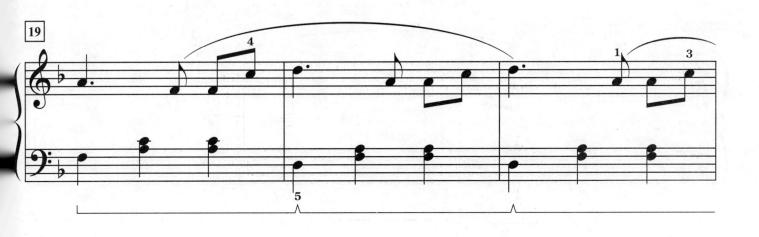

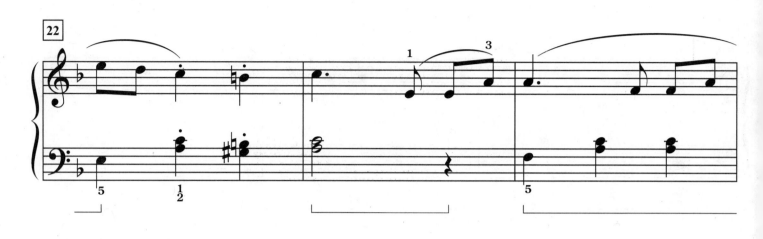

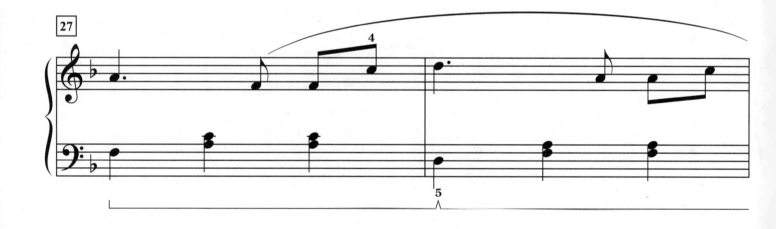

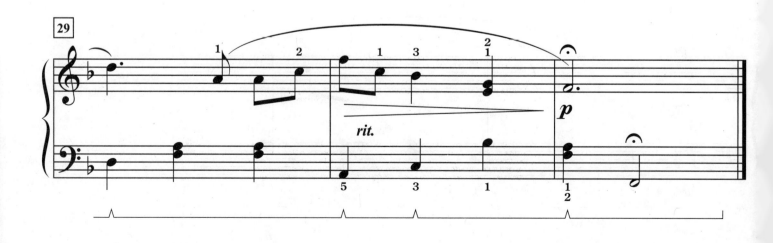

Ballade No. 1

Frédéric Chopin (1810–1849)
Op. 23
Arranged by Jerry Ray

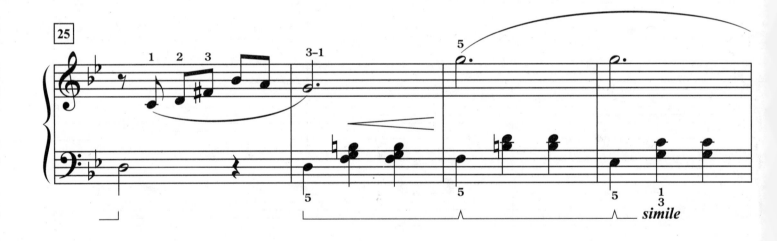

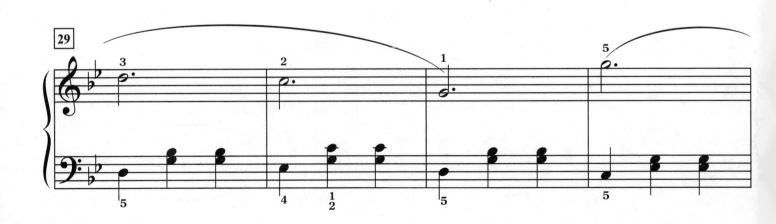

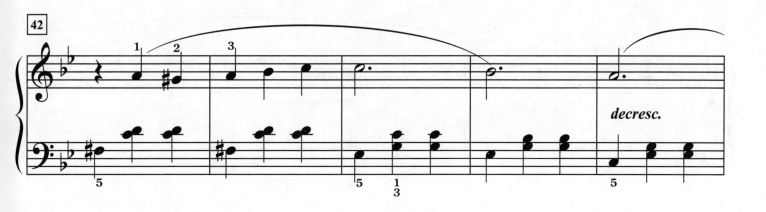

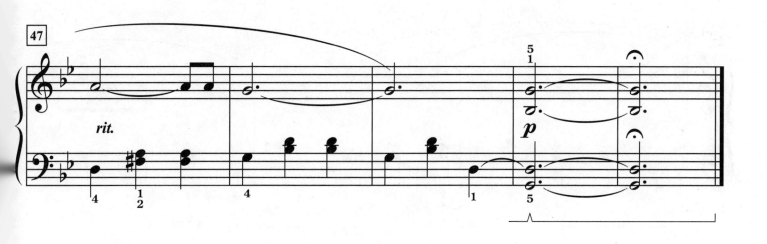

Fantaisie-Impromptu

Frédéric Chopin (1810–1849)
Op. 66
Arranged by Jerry Ray

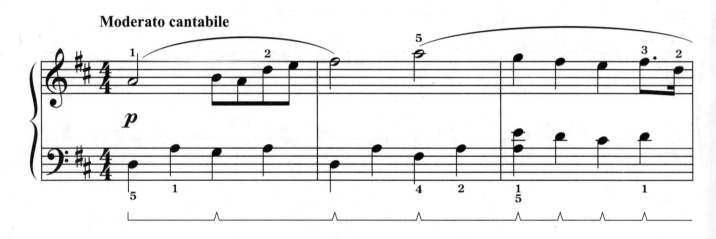

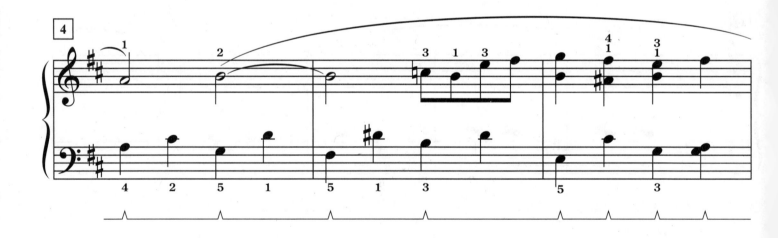

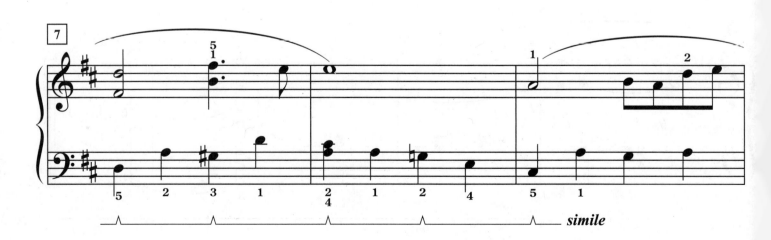

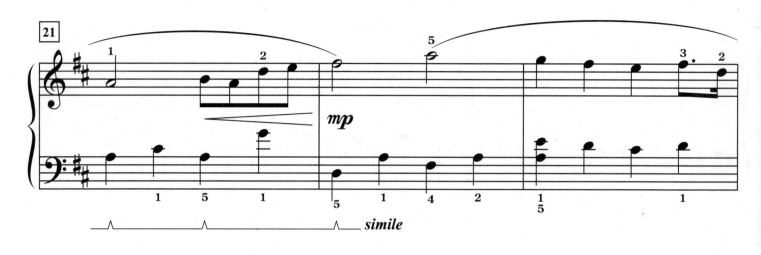

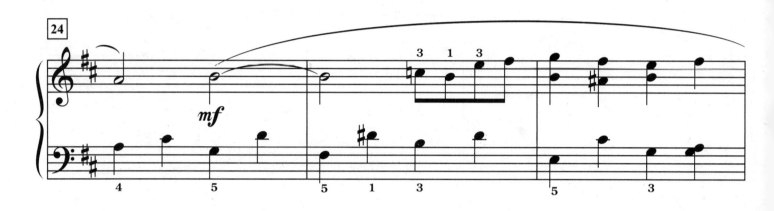

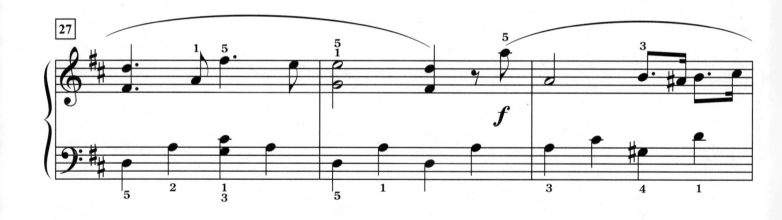

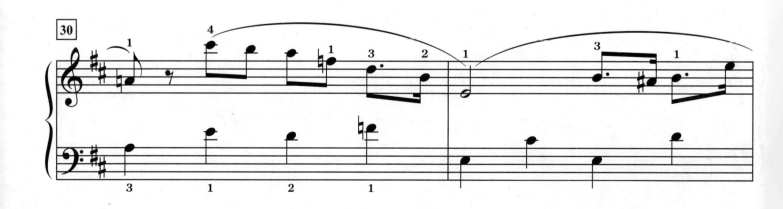

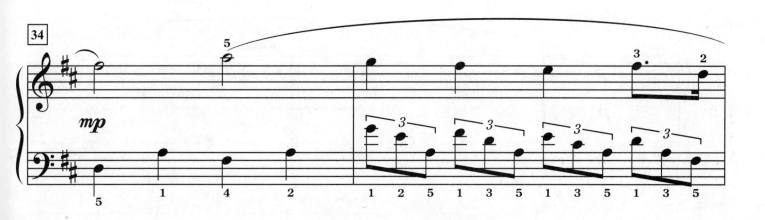

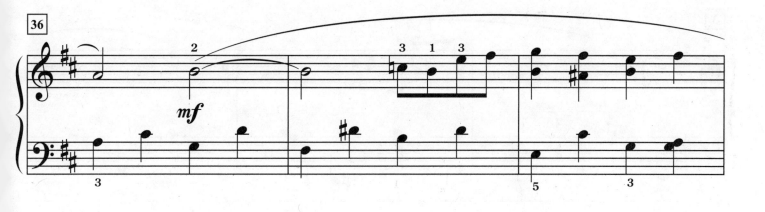

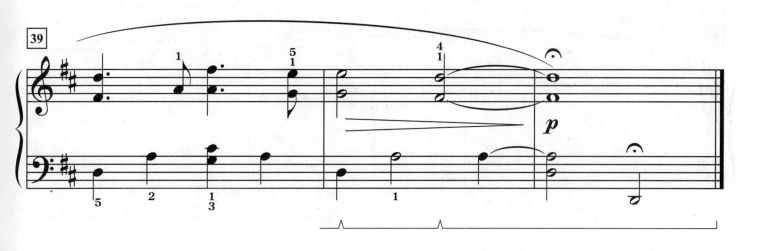

Nocturne

Frédéric Chopin (1810–1849)
Op. 55, No. 1
Arranged by Jerry Ray

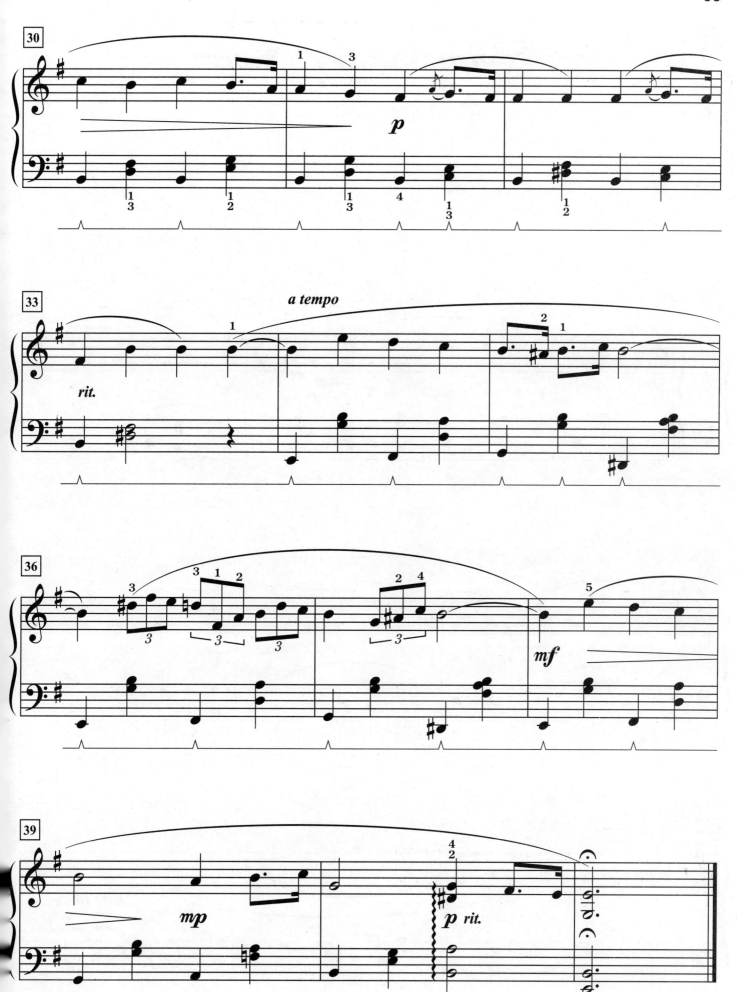

"Revolutionary" Etude

Frédéric Chopin (1810–1849)
Op. 10, No. 12
Arranged by Jerry Ray

Allegro con fuoco

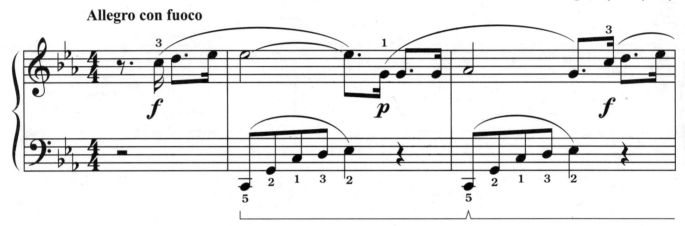

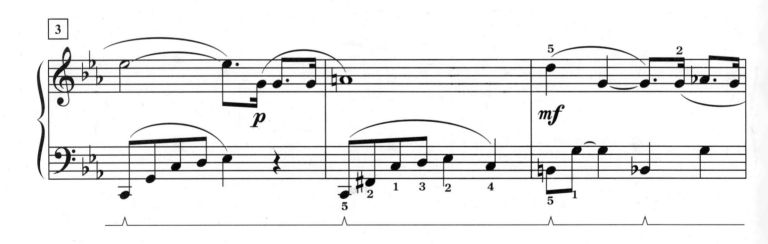

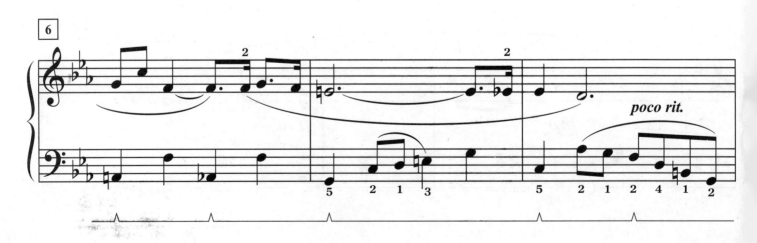

"Funeral March" Sonata

(Sonata No. 2, Third Movement)

Frédéric Chopin (1810–1849)
Op. 35
Arranged by Jerry Ray

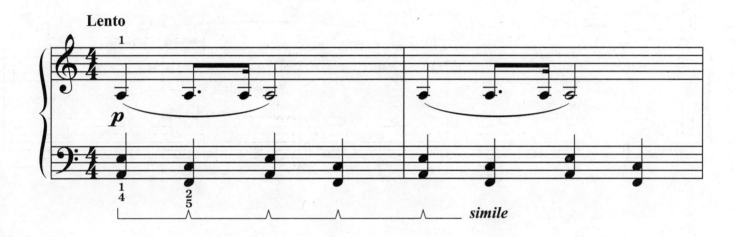

"Raindrop" Prelude

Frédéric Chopin (1810–1849)
Op. 28, No. 15
Arranged by Jerry Ray

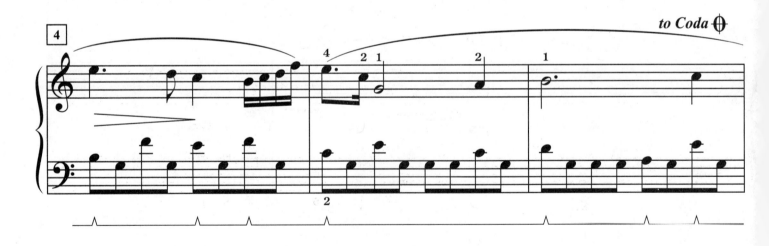

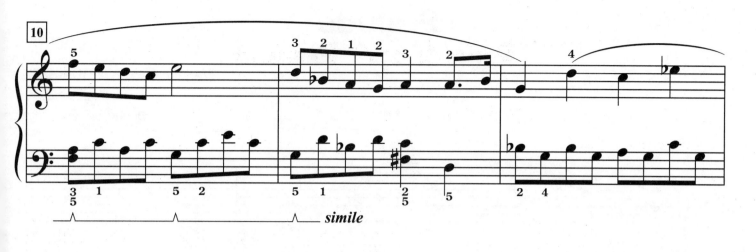

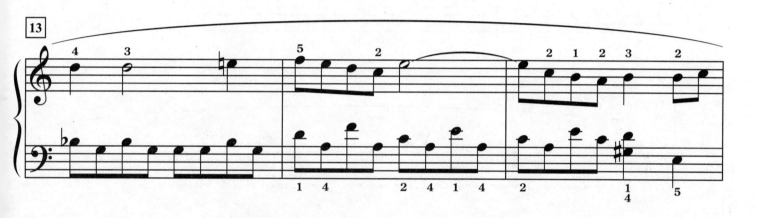

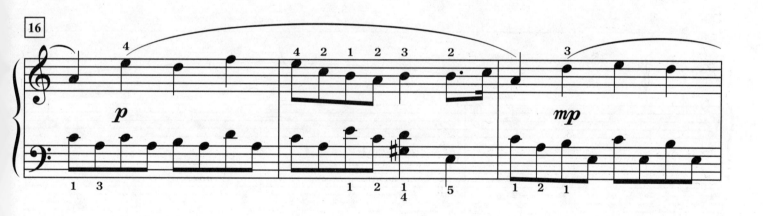

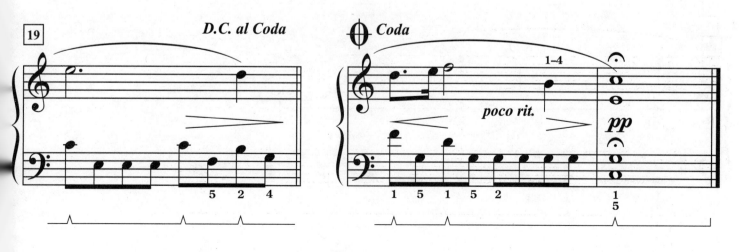

Prelude

Frédéric Chopin (1810–1849)
Op. 28, No. 4
Arranged by Jerry Ray

"Military" Polonaise

Frédéric Chopin (1810–1849)
Op. 40, No. 1
Arranged by Jerry Ray

Allegro con brio

"Minute" Waltz

Frédéric Chopin (1810–1849)
Op. 64, No. 1
Arranged by Jerry Ray

Molto vivace

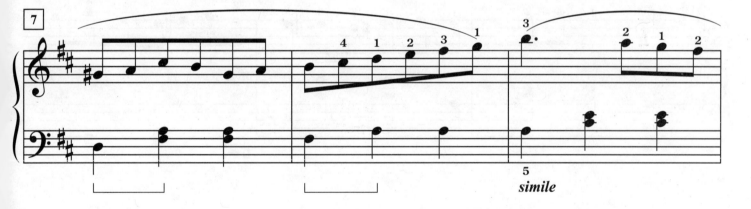

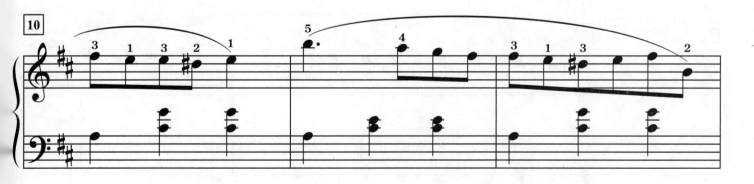

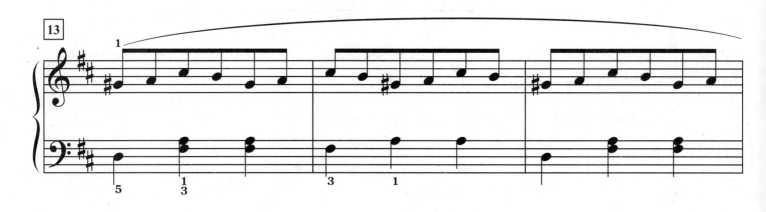

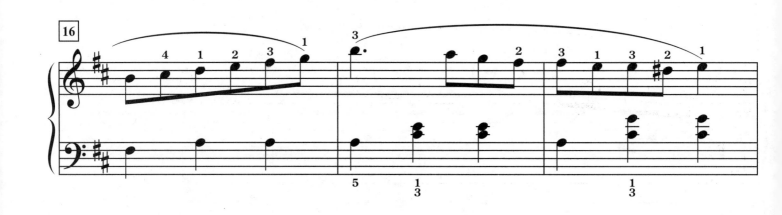

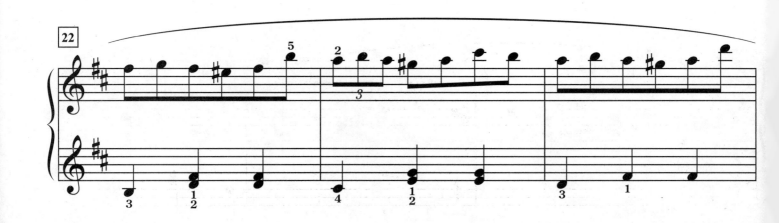

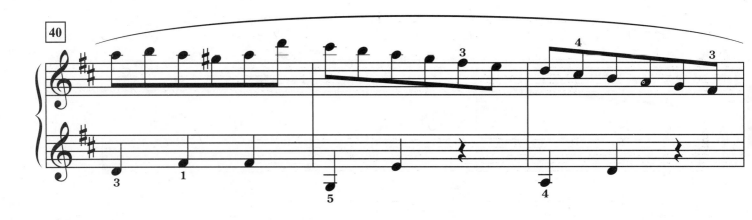

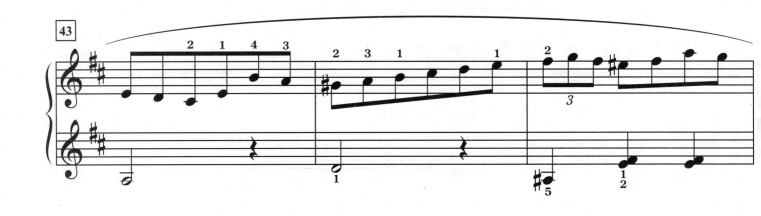

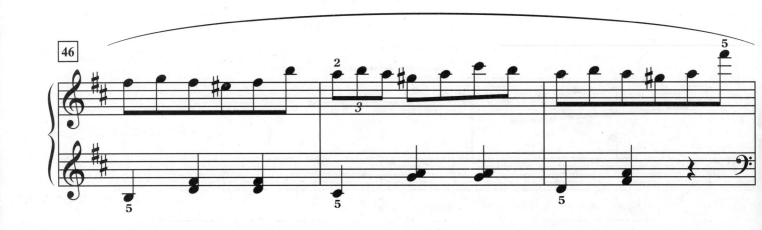

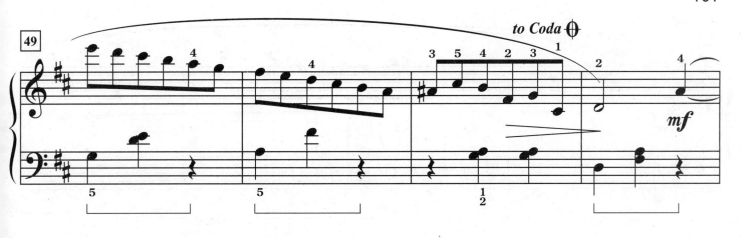

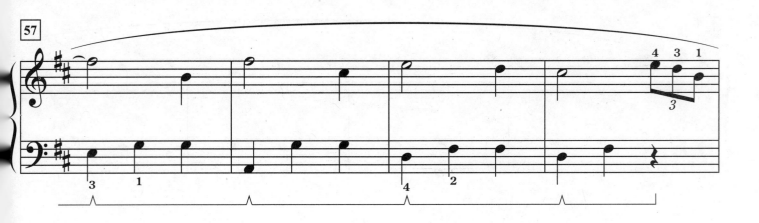

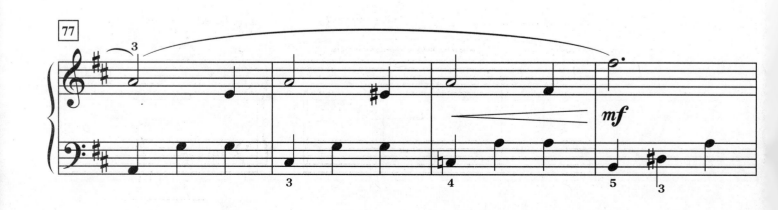

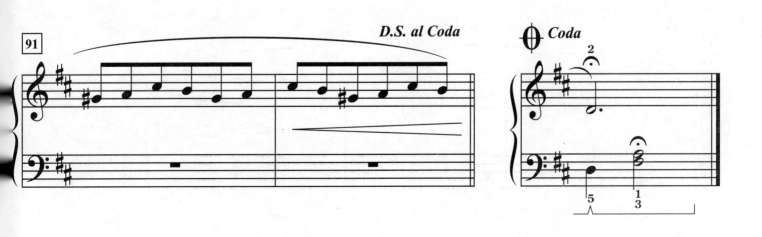

Prince of Denmark's March

Jeremiah Clarke (1673–1707)
Arranged by Bruce Nelson

Maestoso

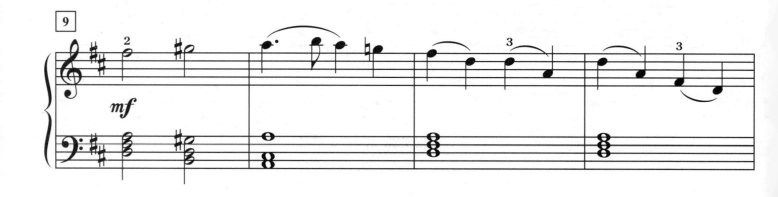

Clair de lune

(from *Suite bergamasque*)

Claude Debussy (1862–1918)
Arranged by E. L. Lancaster

Andaluza No. 5

(from *12 Spanish Dances*)

Enrique Granados (1867–1916)
Arranged by Carol Matz

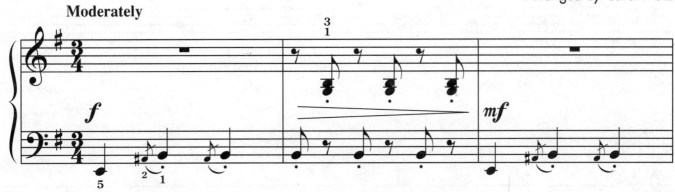

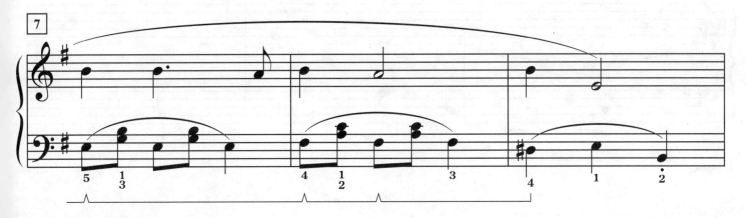

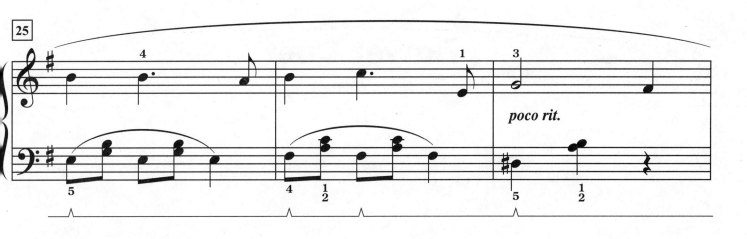

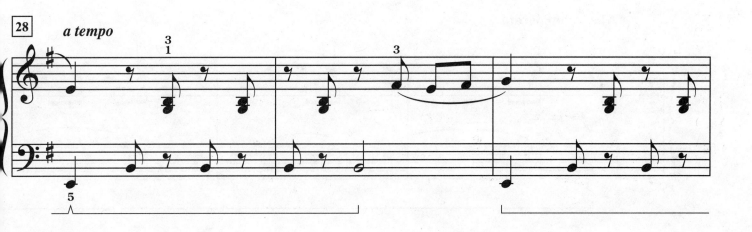

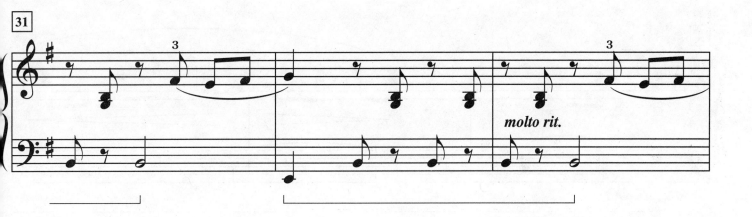

Flower Duet

(from *Lakmé*)

Léo Delibes (1836–1891)
Arranged by Tom Gerou

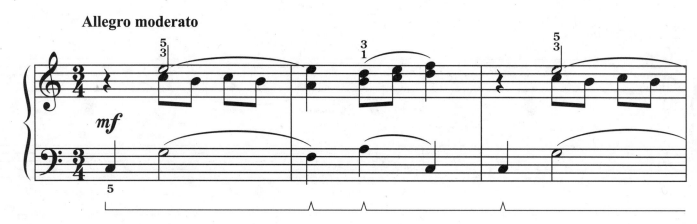

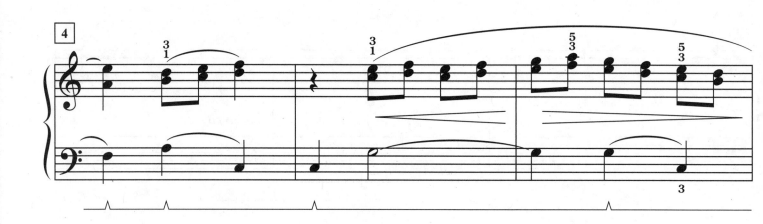

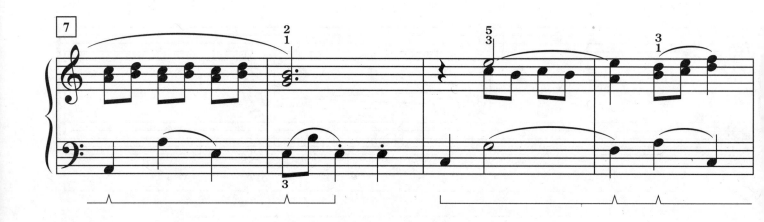

The Sorcerer's Apprentice

Paul Dukas (1865–1935)
Arranged by Robert Schultz

Animato

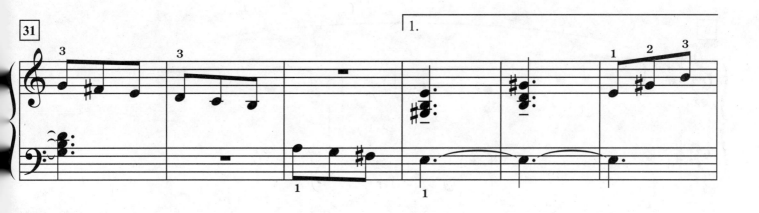

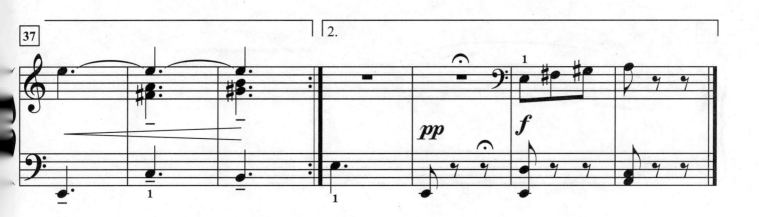

"New World" Symphony

(Symphony No. 9, Second Movement)

Antonín Dvořák (1841–1904)
Op. 95
Arranged by Robert Schultz

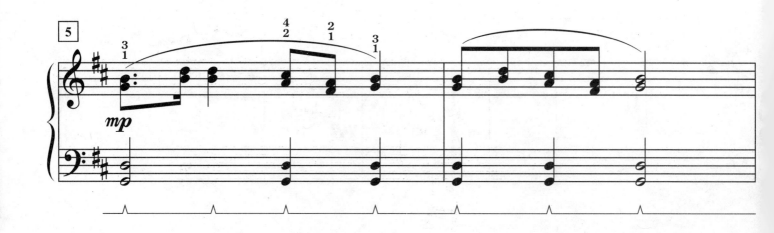

Pomp and Circumstance

(March No. 1)

Edward Elgar (1857–1934)
Op. 39
Arranged by Robert Schultz

Largamente

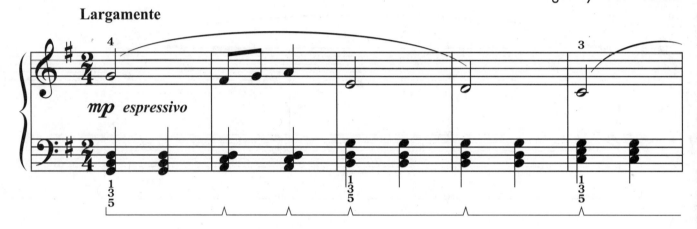

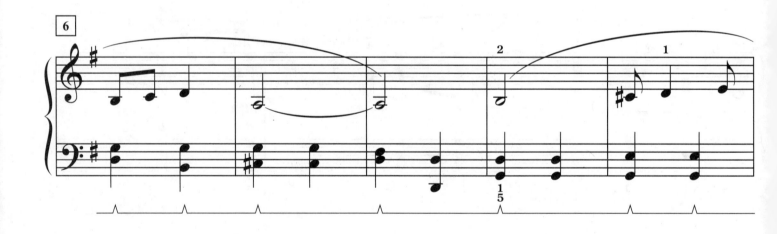

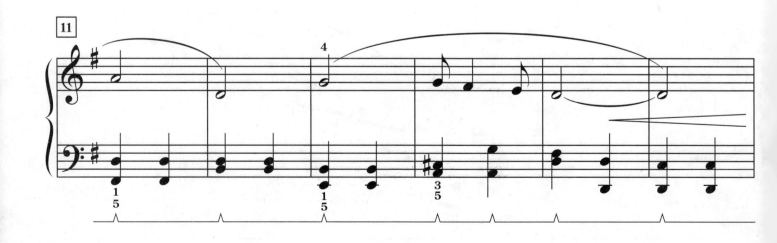

Pavane

Gabriel Fauré (1845–1924)
Op. 50
Arranged by Robert Schultz

Allegro moderato

Ave Maria

Johann Sebastian Bach (1685–1750)
Charles Gounod (1818–1893)
Arranged by Jerry Ray

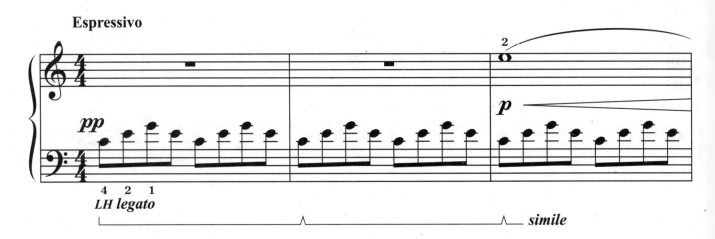

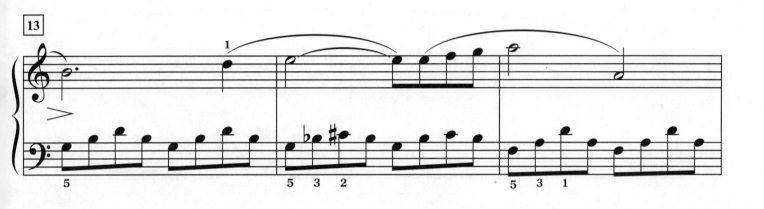

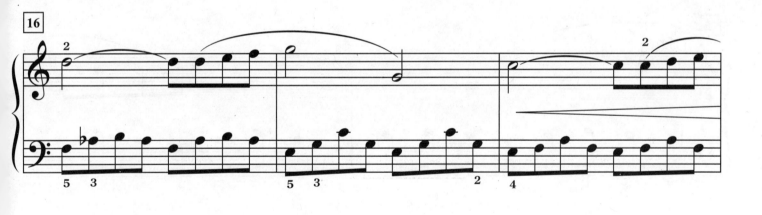

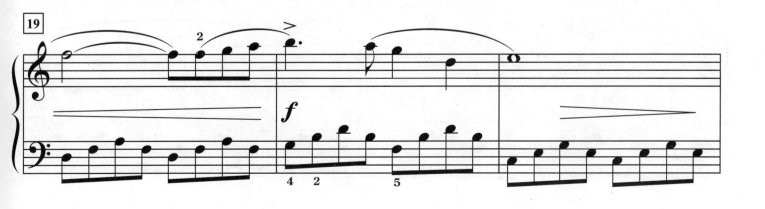

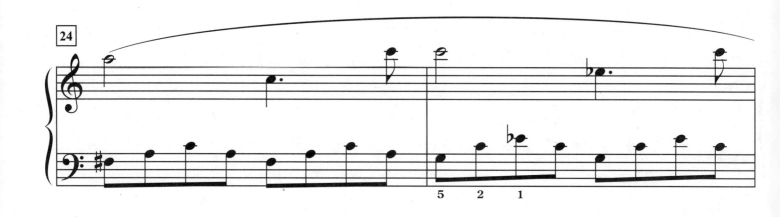

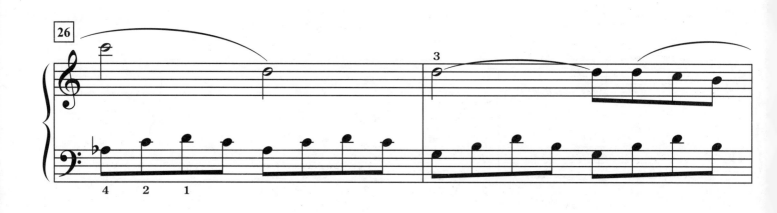

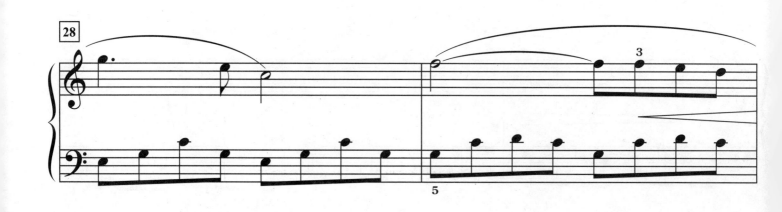

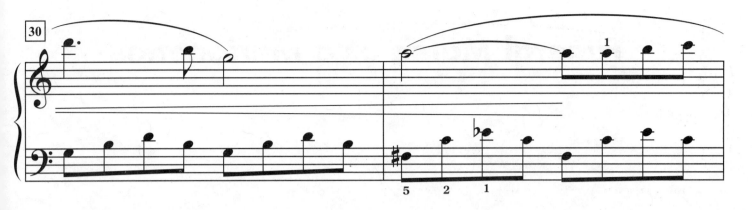

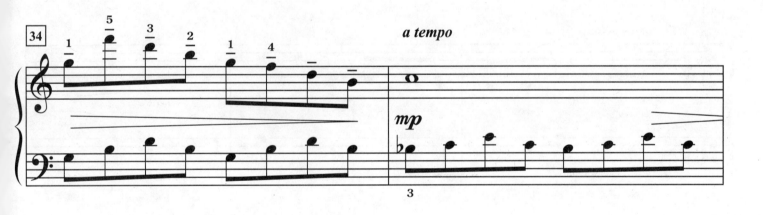

Funeral March of a Marionette

Charles Gounod (1818–1893)
Arranged by Carol Matz

Moderately

In the Hall of the Mountain King

(from *Peer Gynt Suite No. 1*)

Edvard Grieg (1843–1907)
Op. 46, No. 4
Arranged by Carol Matz

Moderately fast

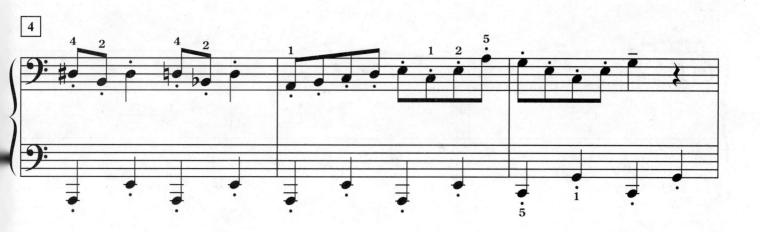

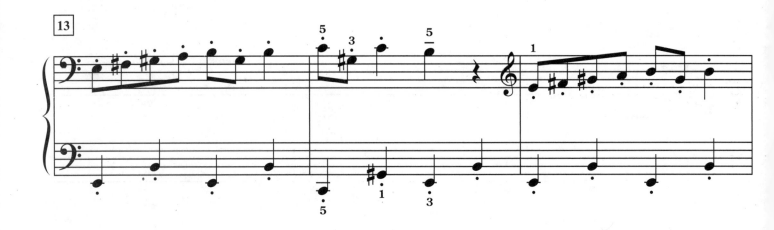

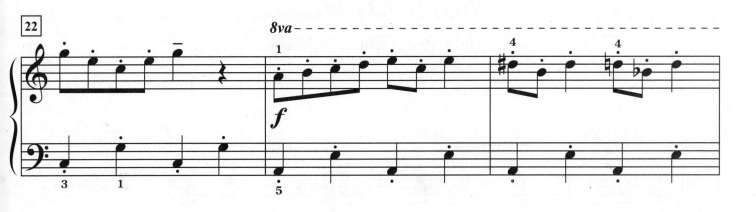

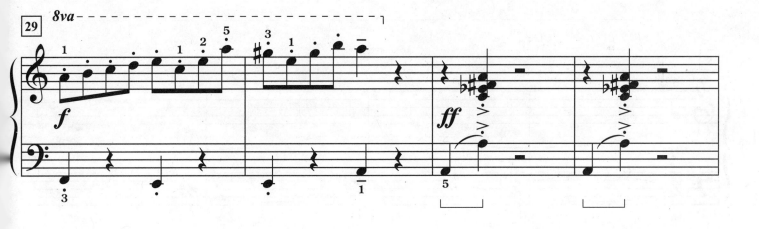

Morning Mood

(from *Peer Gynt Suite No. 1*)

Edvard Grieg (1843–1907)
Op. 46, No. 1
Arranged by Carol Matz

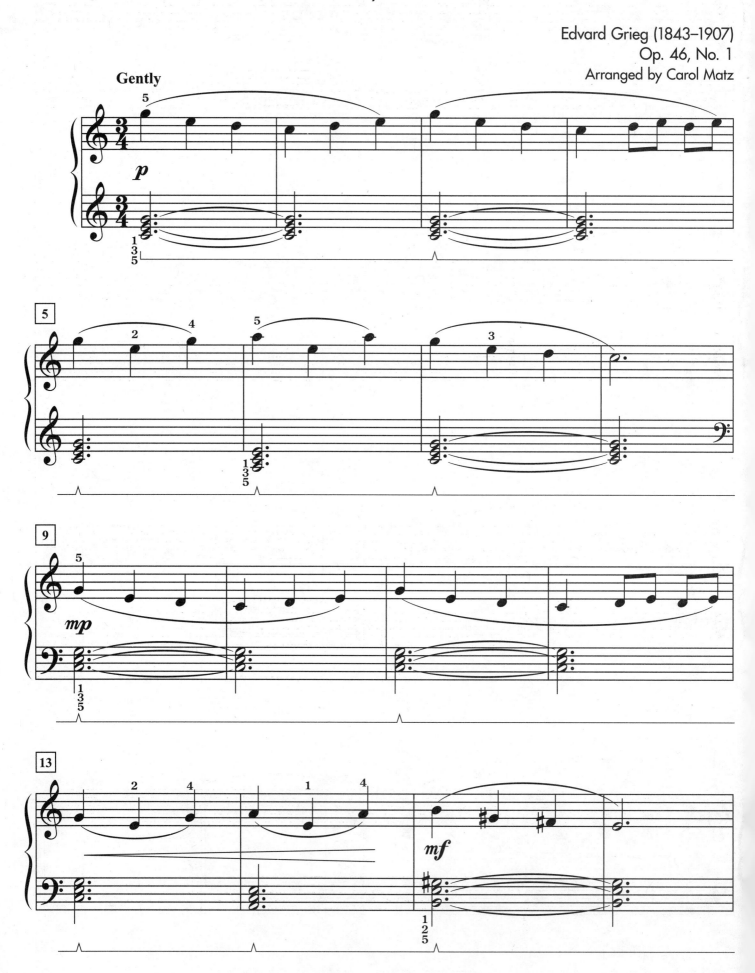

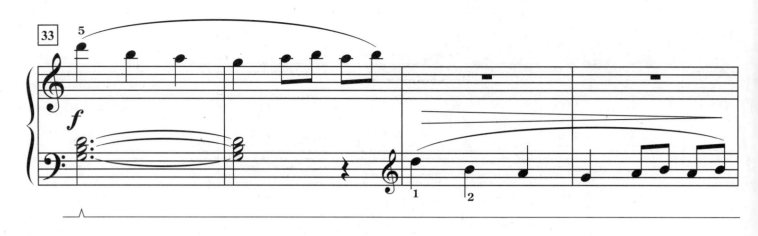

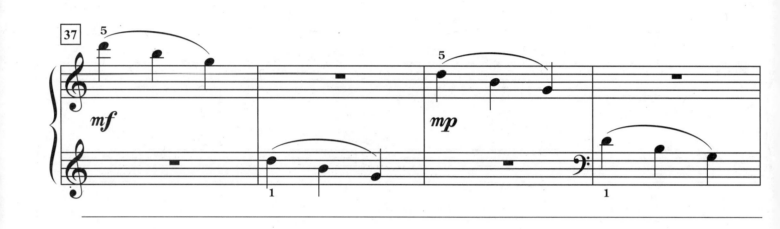

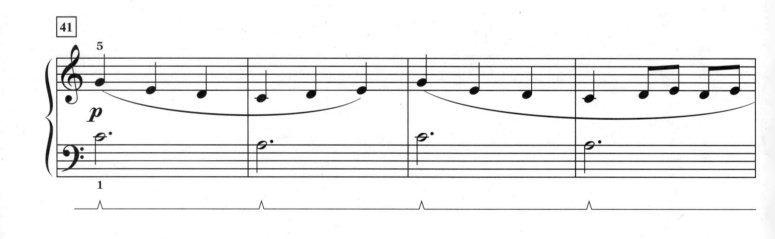

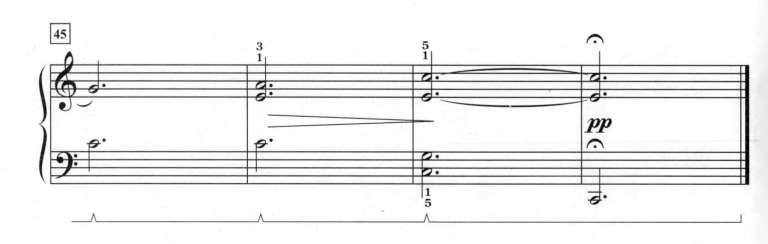

Hallelujah Chorus

(from *Messiah*)

George Frideric Handel (1685–1759)
HWV 56
Arranged by Bruce Nelson

Hal - le - lu - jah! Hal - le - lu - jah! Hal - le -

lu - jah! Hal - le - lu - jah! Hal - le - lu - jah! Hal - le - lu - jah!

Hal - le - lu - jah! Hal - le - lu - jah! Hal - le - lu - jah! Hal - le - lu - jah!

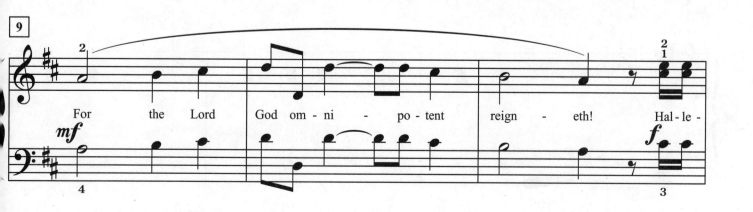

For the Lord God om - ni - po - tent reign - eth! Hal - le -

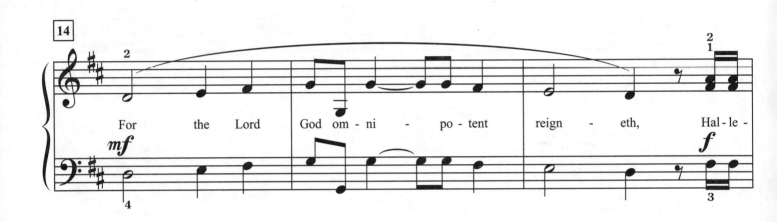

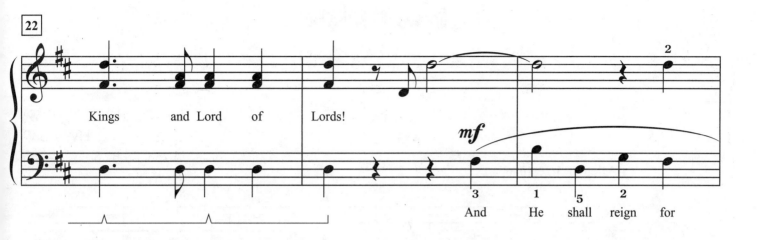

Kings and Lord of Lords!

mf

And He shall reign for

f

For - ev - er and ev - er! For - ev - er and

ev - er and ev - er!

ev - er! Hal - le - lu - jah! Hal - le - lu - jah! Hal - le - lu - jah! Hal - le -

cresc.

lu - jah! Hal - le - lu jah!

ff

Hornpipe

(from *Water Music*)

George Frideric Handel (1685–1759)
HWV 349
Arranged by Bruce Nelson

Allegro maestoso

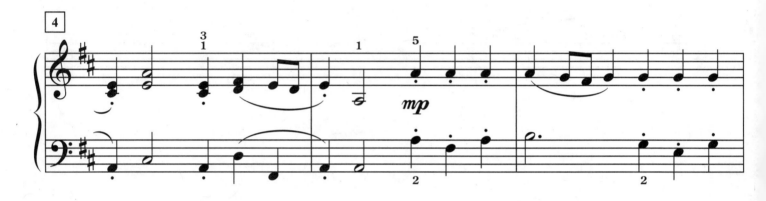

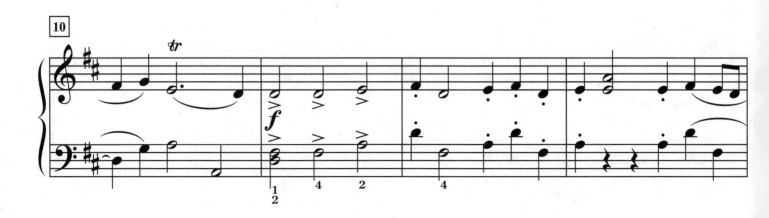

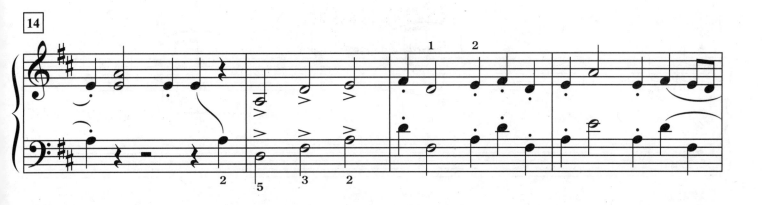

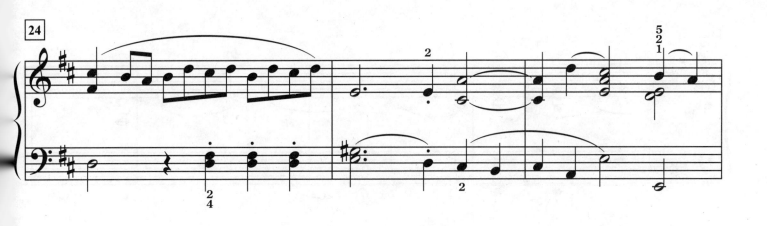

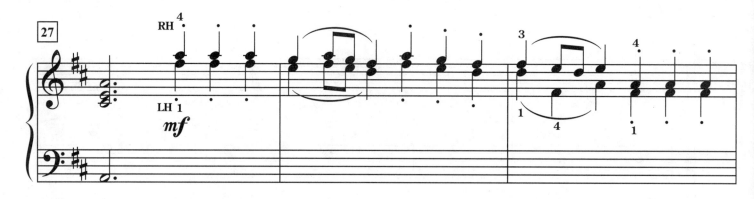

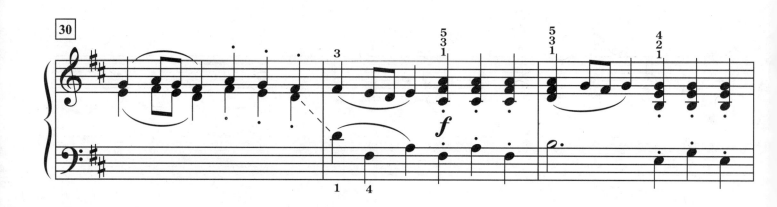

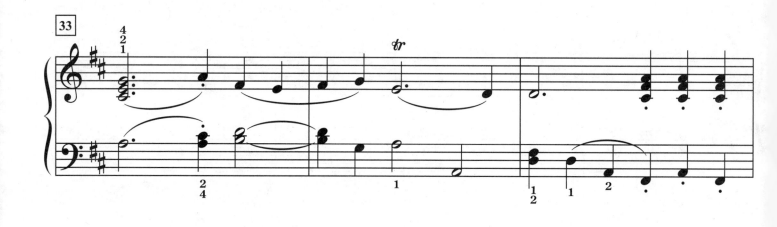

Solace

(A Mexican Serenade)

Scott Joplin (1868–1917)
Arranged by Mary Sallee

Very slow march time

both hands sempre legato

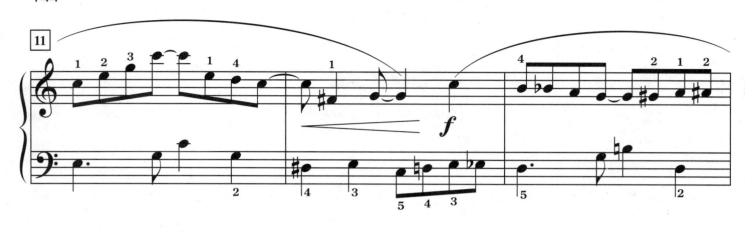

The Entertainer

Scott Joplin (1868–1917)
Arranged by Mary Sallee

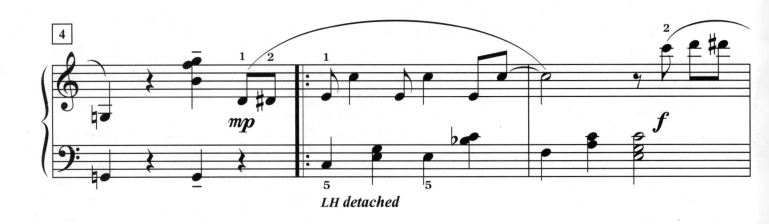

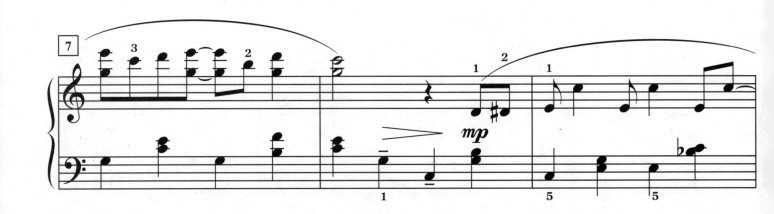

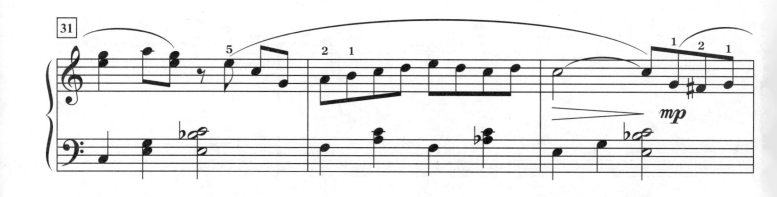

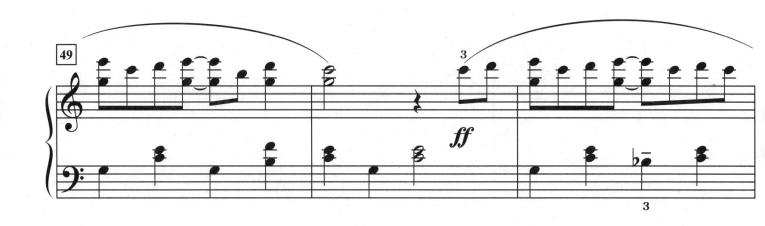

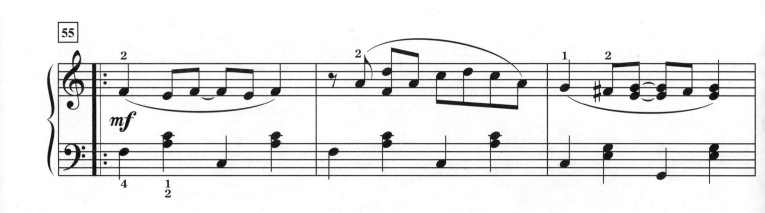

Maple Leaf Rag

Scott Joplin (1868–1917)
Arranged by Mary Sallee

158

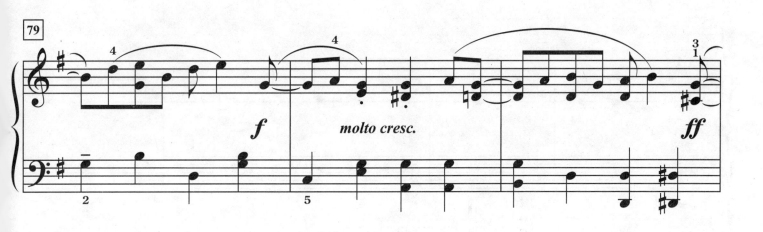

"Surprise" Symphony

(Symphony No. 94, Second Movement)

Franz Joseph Haydn (1732–1809)
H. 94
Arranged by Robert Schultz

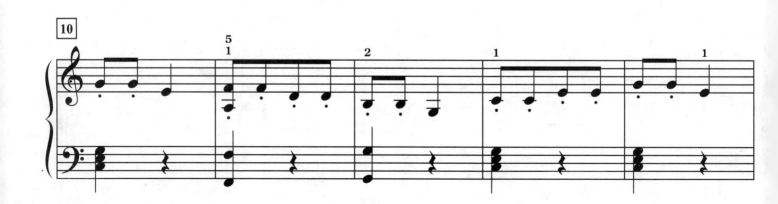

Waltz

(from *The Merry Widow*)

Franz Lehár (1870–1948)
Arranged by Robert Schultz

Moderato

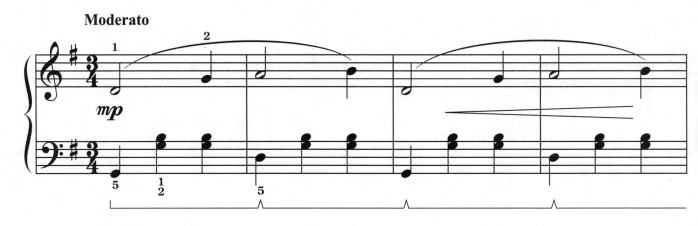

simile

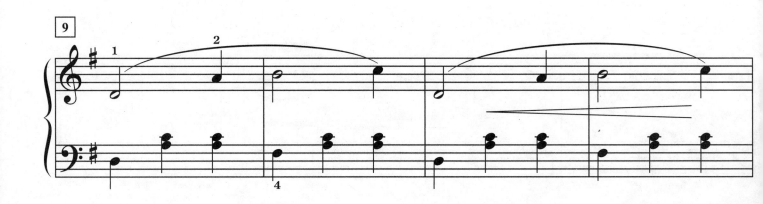

Intermezzo

(from *Cavalleria rusticana*)

Pietro Mascagni (1863–1945)
Arranged by Tom Gerou

Meditation

(from *Thaïs*)

Jules Massenet (1842–1912)
Arranged by Tom Gerou

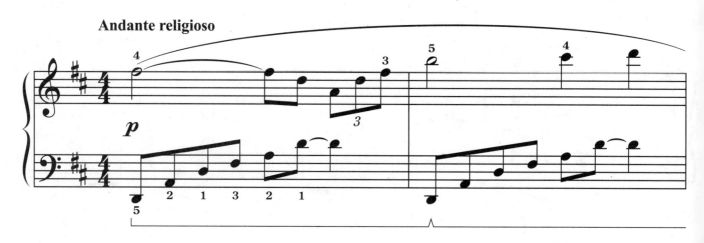

Wedding March

(from *A Midsummer Night's Dream*)

Felix Mendelssohn (1809–1847)
Op. 21
Arranged by Robert Schultz

Rondeau

(from *Suite de symphonies*)

Jean-Joseph Mouret (1682–1738)
Arranged by Bruce Nelson

Allegro maestoso

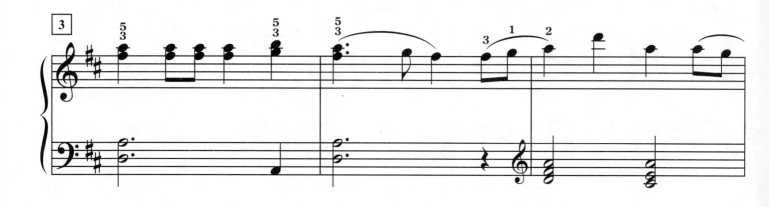

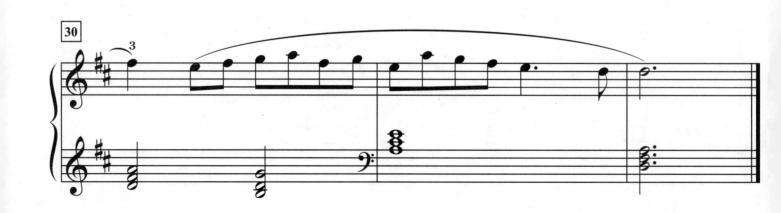

Eine kleine Nachtmusik

(First Movement)

Wolfgang Amadeus Mozart (1756–1791)
K. 525
Arranged by Mary K. Sallee

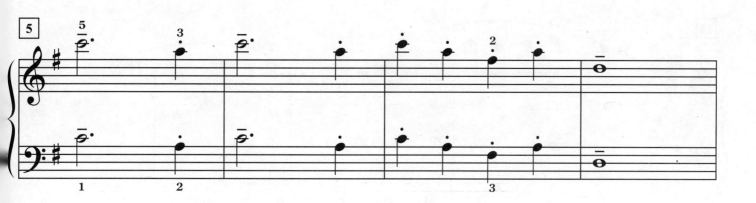

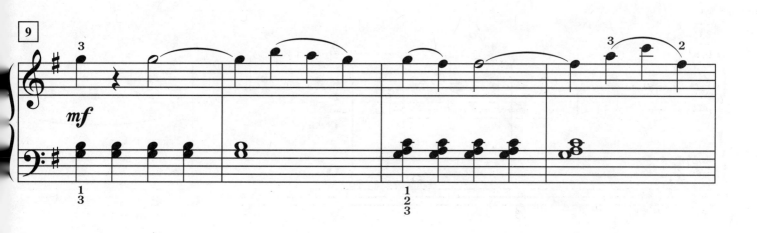

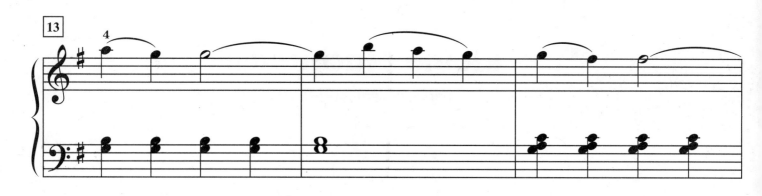

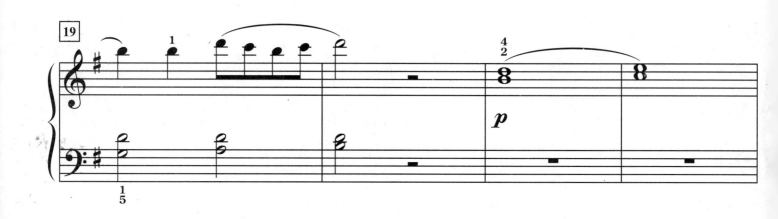

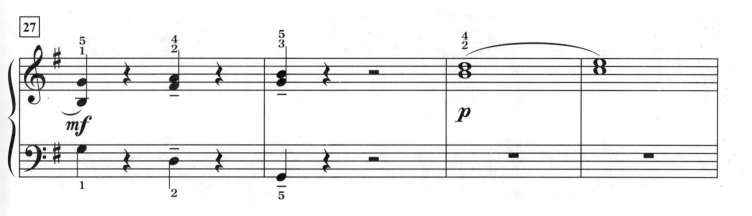

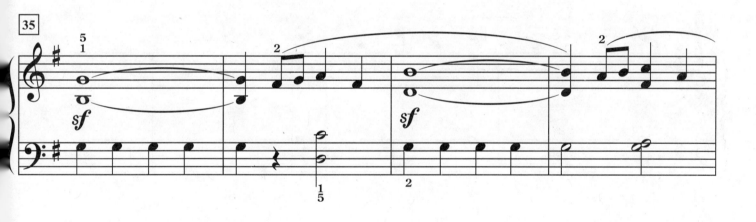

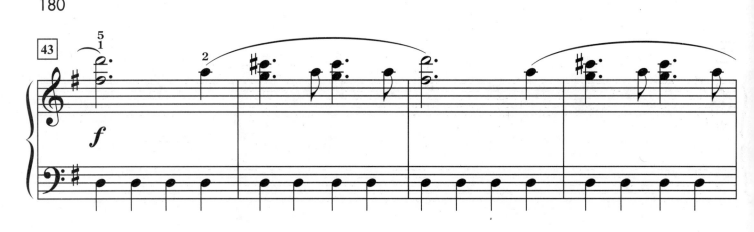

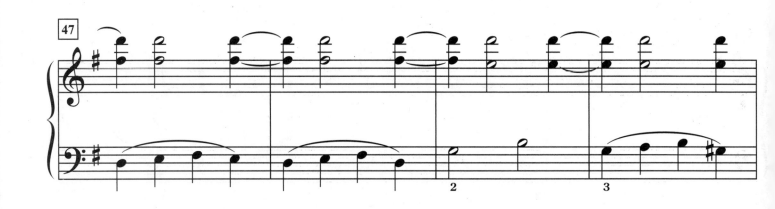

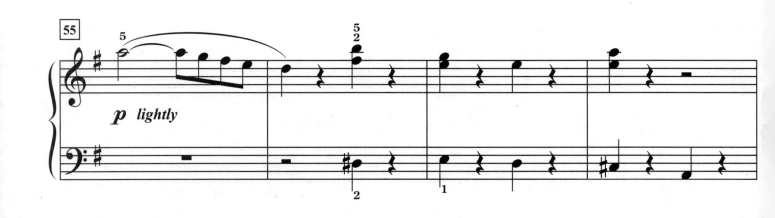

Variations on "Ah, vous dirai-je, Maman"

French Folk Song
Variations by Wolfgang Amadeus Mozart (1756–1791)
K. 265
Arranged by Jerry Ray

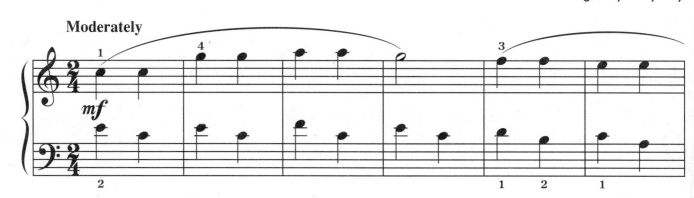

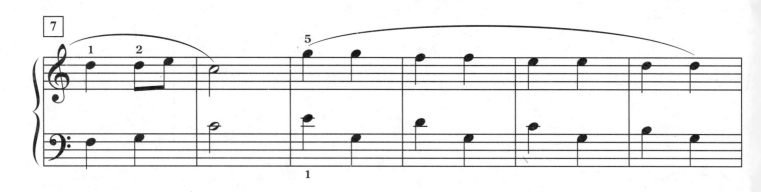

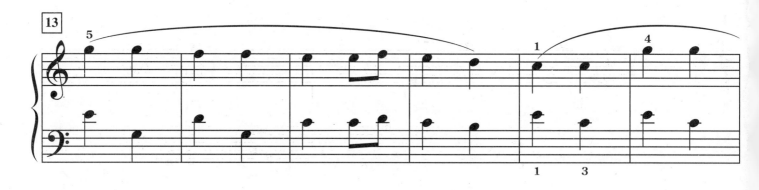

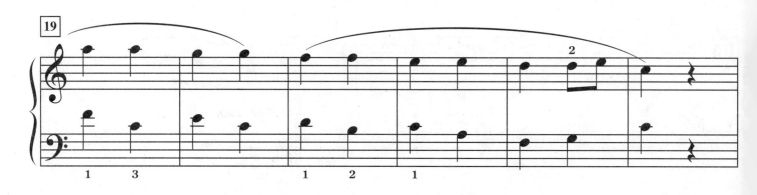

Là ci darem la mano

(from *Don Giovanni*)

Wolfgang Amadeus Mozart (1756–1791)
K. 527
Arranged by Tom Gerou

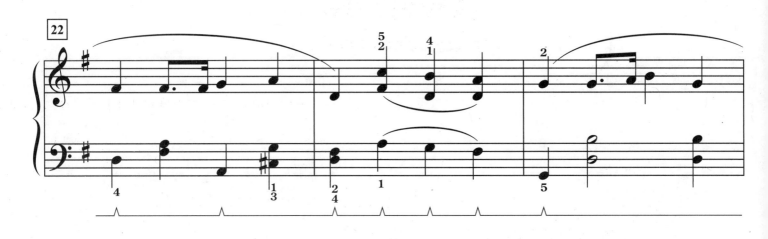

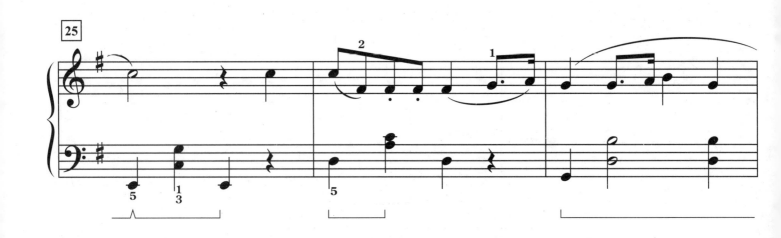

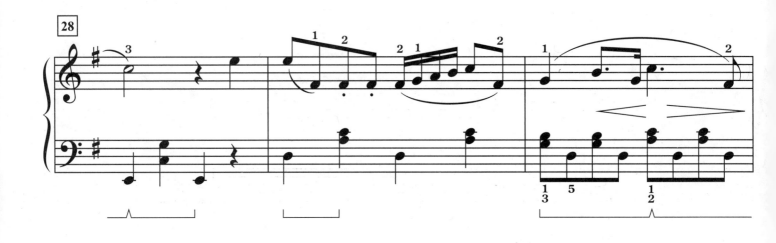

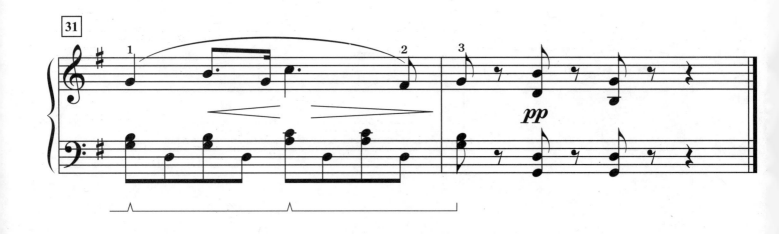

Overture

(from *The Marriage of Figaro*)

Wolfgang Amadeus Mozart (1756–1791)
K. 492
Arranged by Jerry Ray

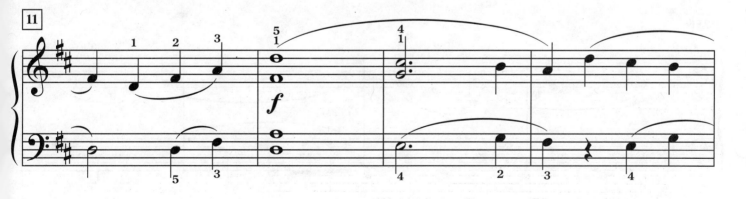

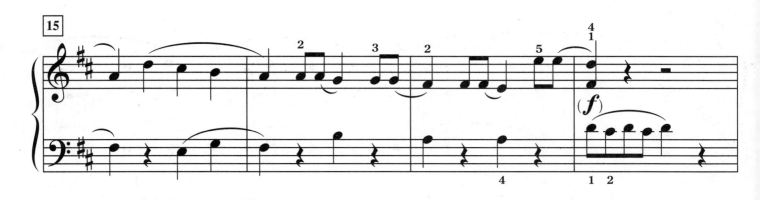

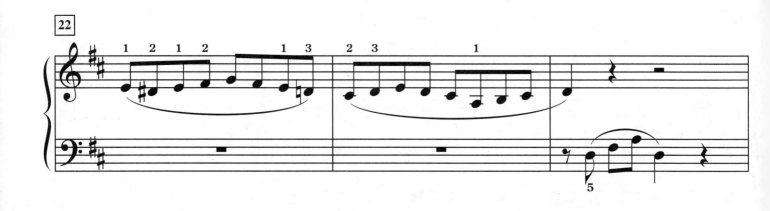

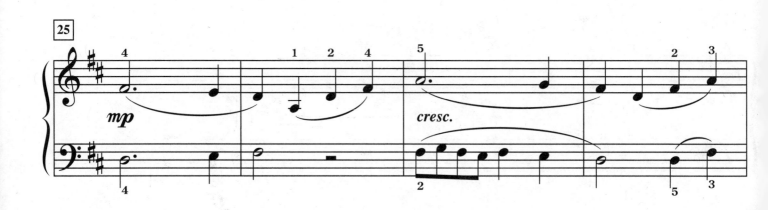

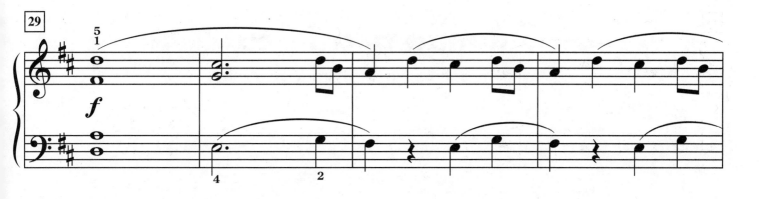

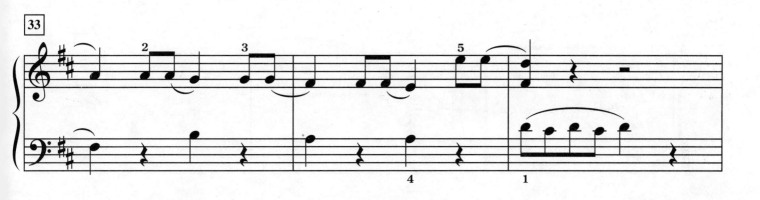

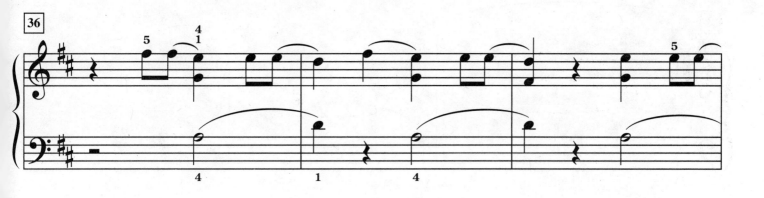

Rondo alla Turca

(Piano Sonata No. 11, Third Movement)

Wolfgang Amadeus Mozart (1756–1791)
K. 331
Arranged by Mary K. Sallee

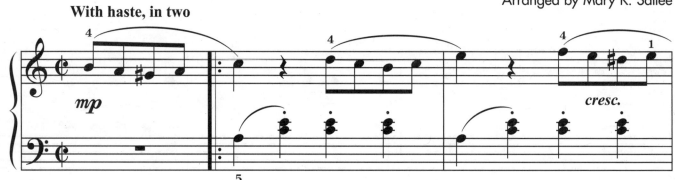

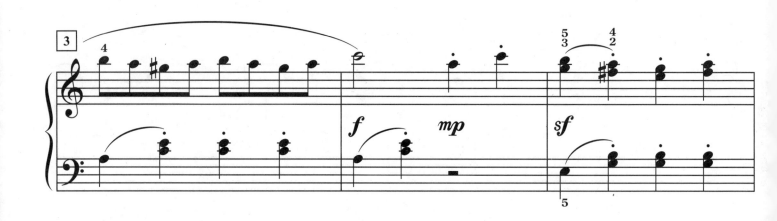

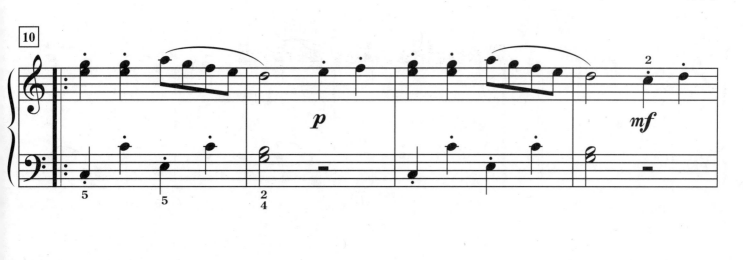

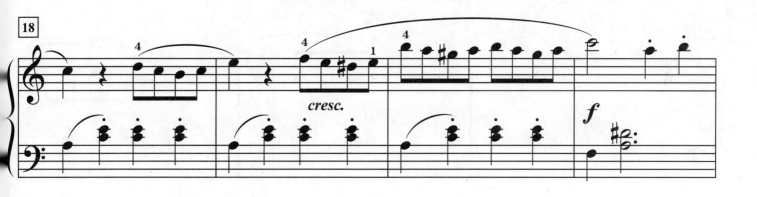

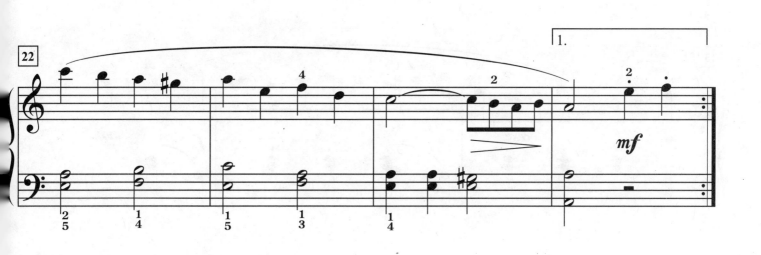

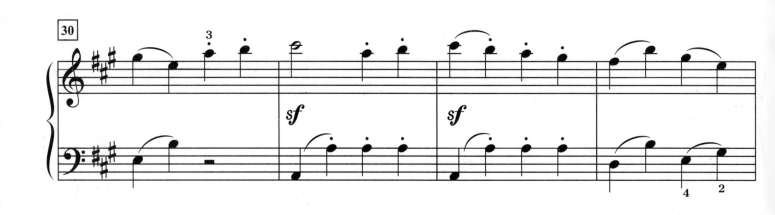

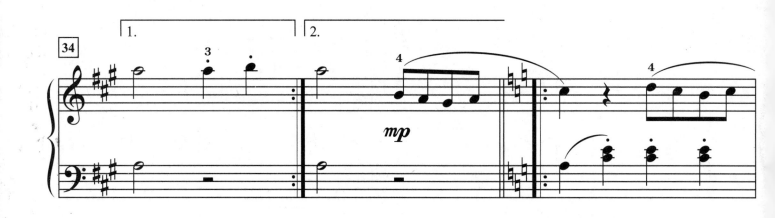

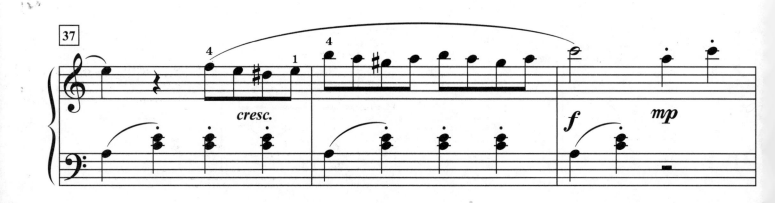

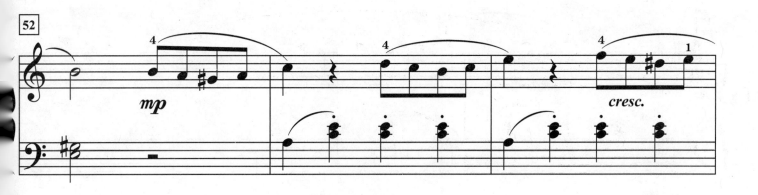

Symphony No. 40

(First Movement)

Wolfgang Amadeus Mozart (1756–1791)
K. 550
Arranged by Robert Schultz

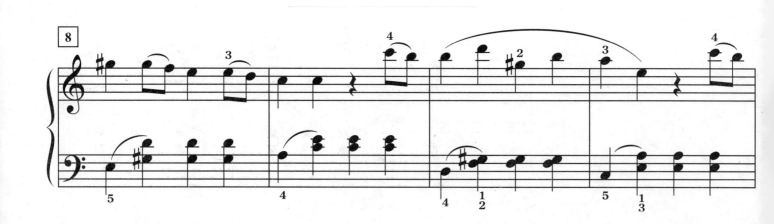

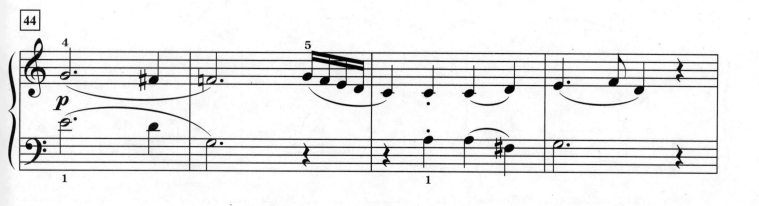

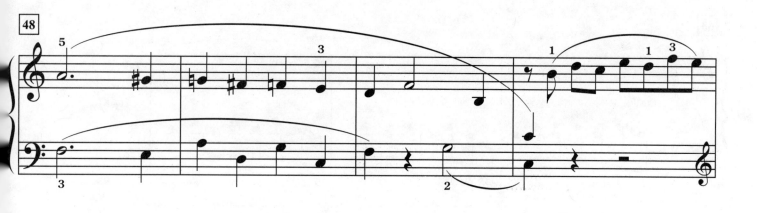

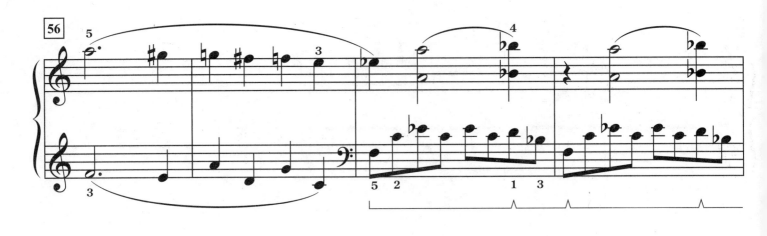

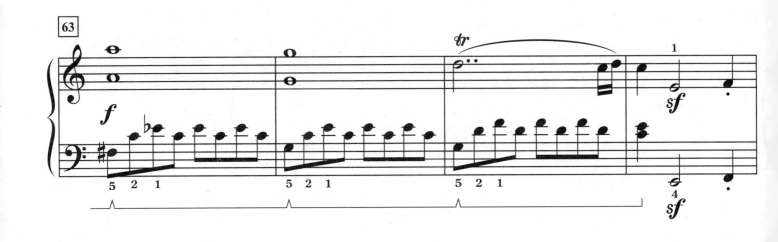

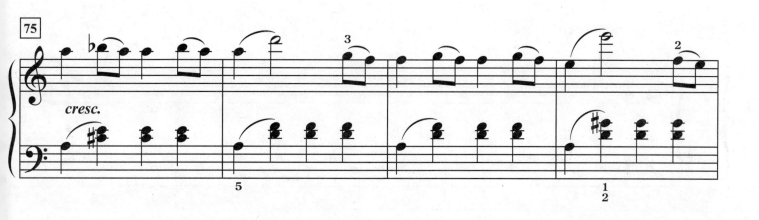

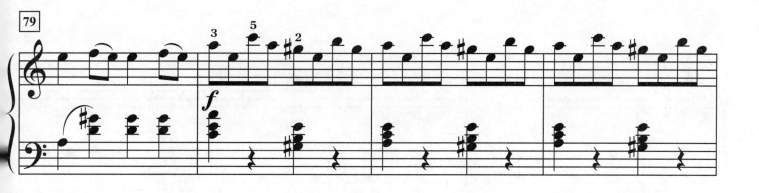

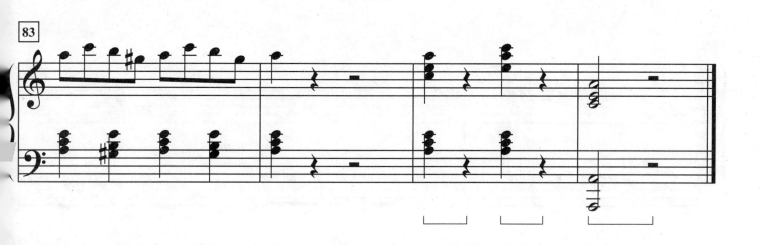

Voi, che sapete

(from *The Marriage of Figaro*)

Wolfgang Amadeus Mozart (1756–1791)
K. 492
Arranged by Tom Gerou

Andante con moto

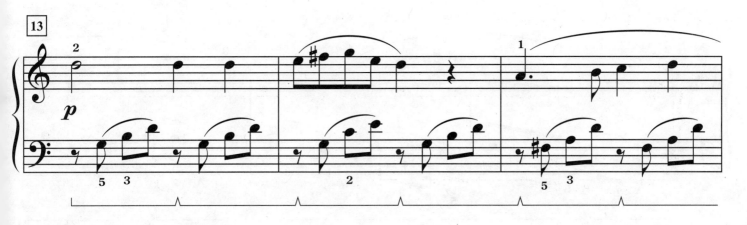

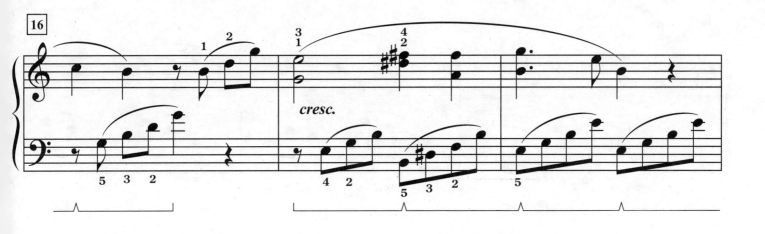

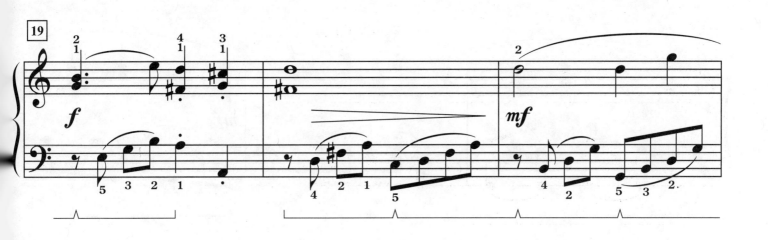

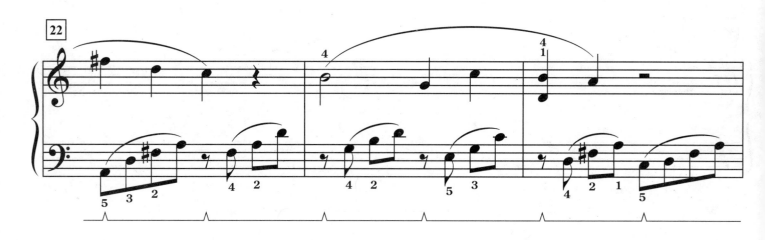

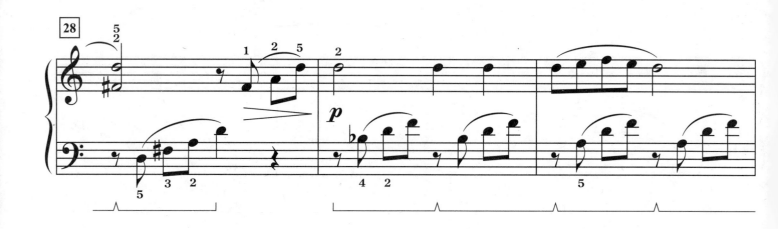

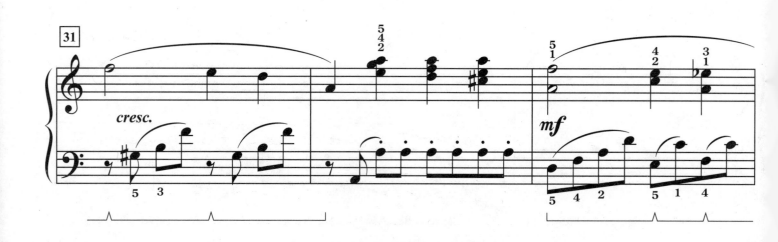

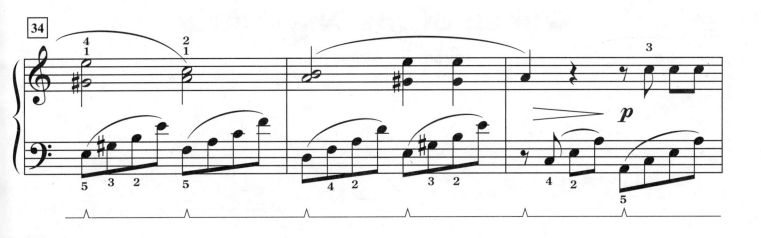

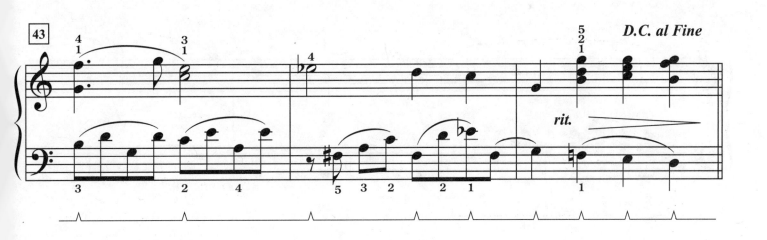

Queen of the Night Aria

(from *The Magic Flute*)

Wolfgang Amadeus Mozart (1756–1791)

K. 620

Arranged by Tom Gerou

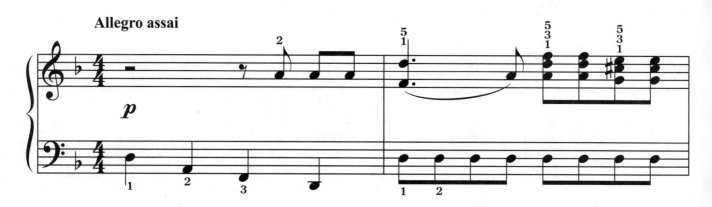

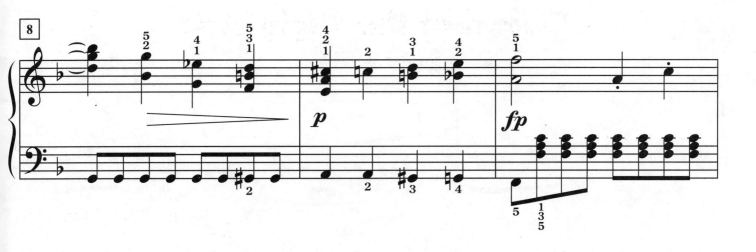

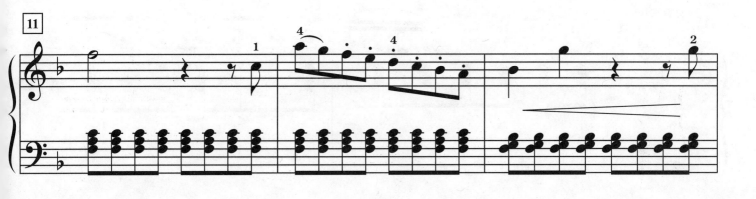

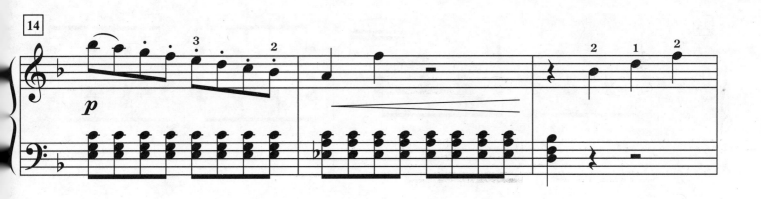

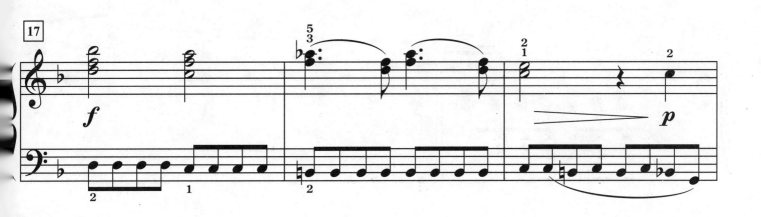

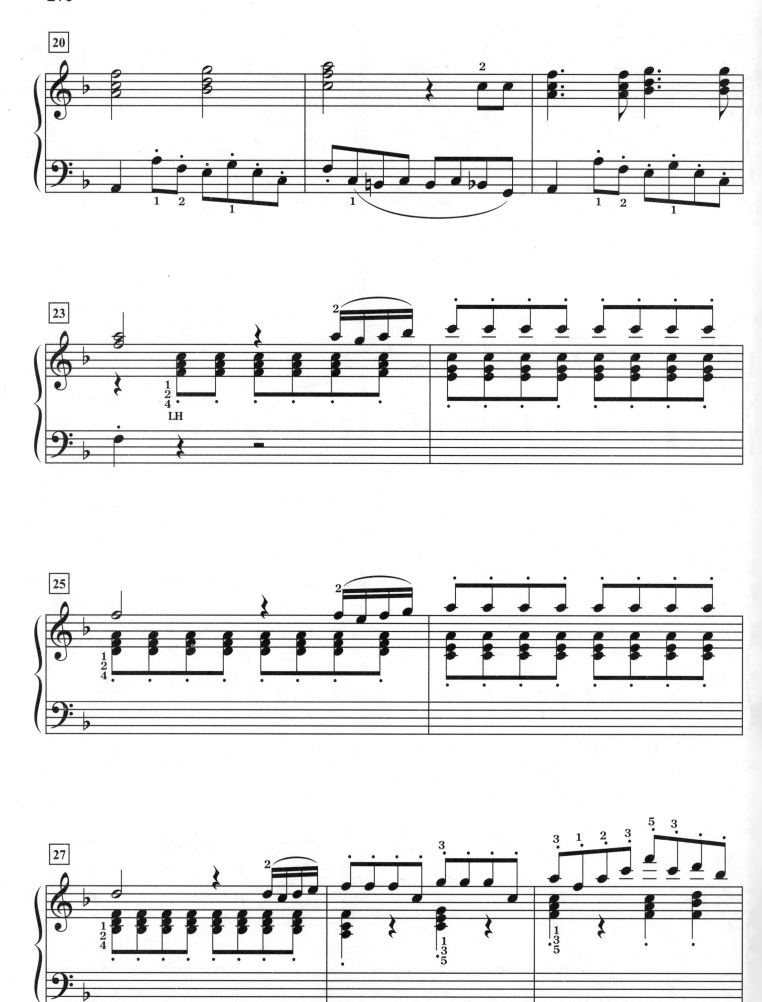

Piano Sonata No. 11

(First Movement)

Wolfgang Amadeus Mozart (1756–1791)
K. 331
Arranged by Jerry Ray

Moderately

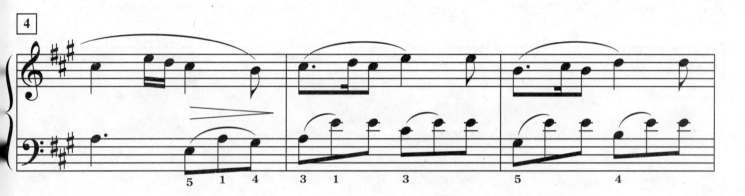

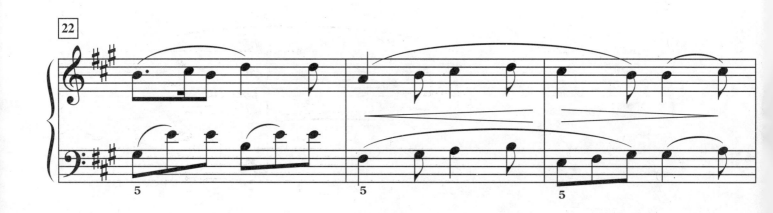

Barcarolle

(from *Tales of Hoffmann*)

Jacques Offenbach (1819–1880)
Arranged by Tom Gerou

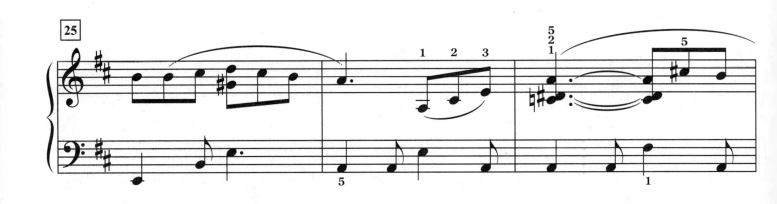

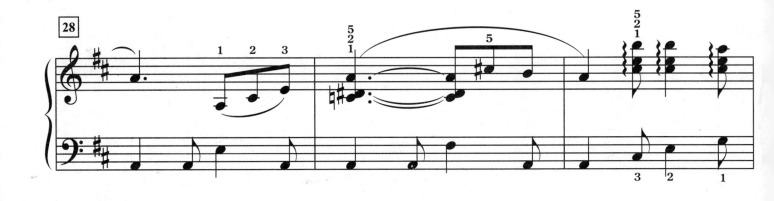

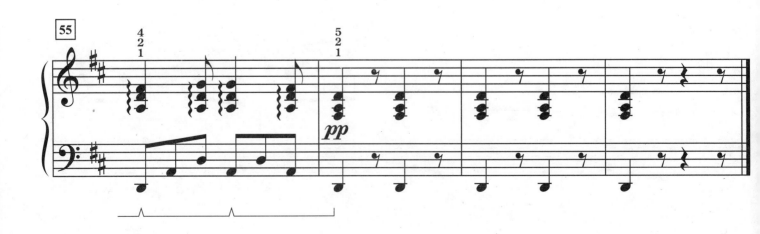

Can-Can

(from *Orpheus in the Underworld*)

Jacques Offenbach (1819–1880)
Arranged by Carol Matz

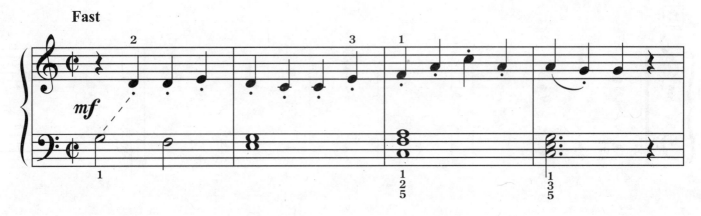

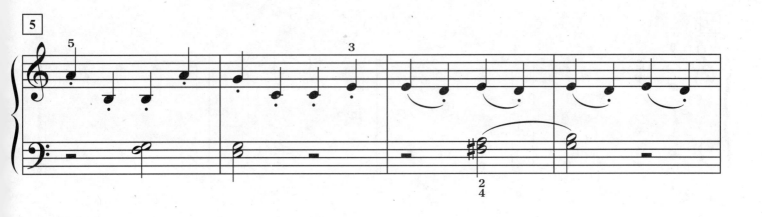

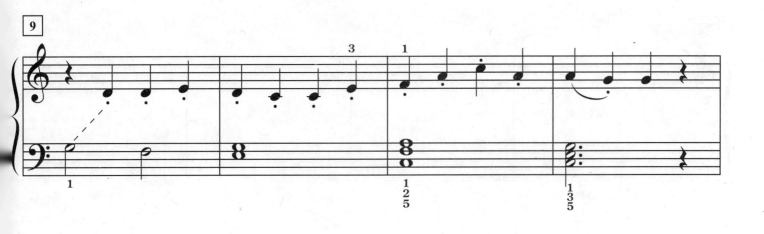

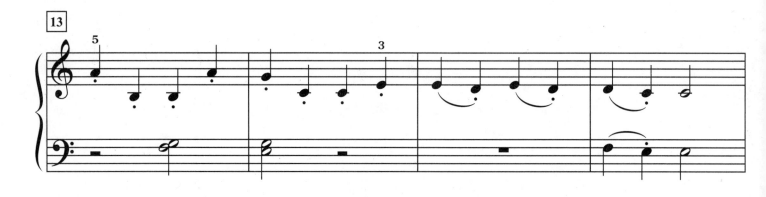

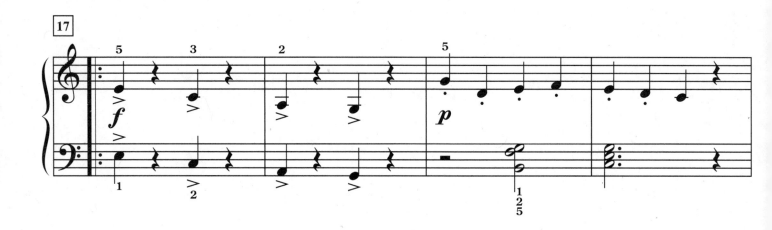

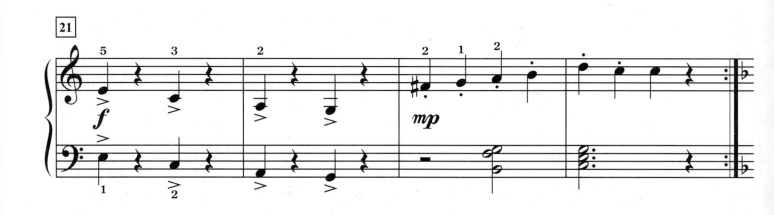

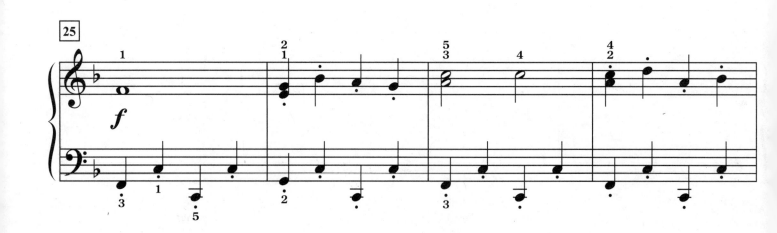

Canon in D

Johann Pachelbel (1653–1706)
Arranged by Bruce Nelson

Andante

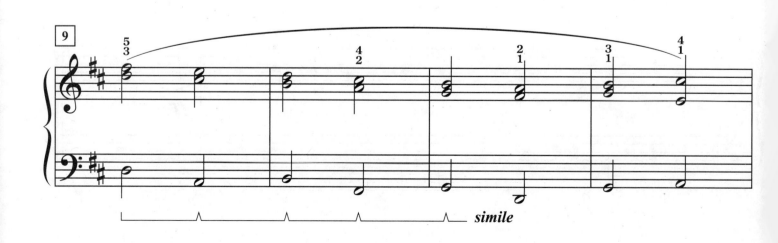

simile

Musetta's Waltz

(from *La bohème*)

Giacomo Puccini (1858–1924)
Arranged by Tom Gerou

Tempo di valse lento

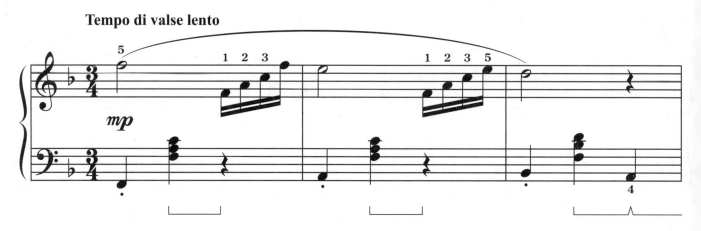

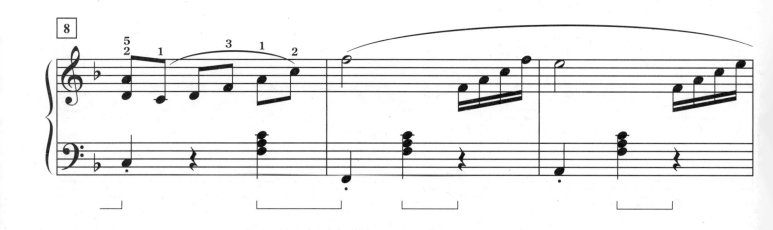

230

O mio babbino caro

(from *Gianni Schicchi*)

Giacomo Puccini (1858–1924)
Arranged by Tom Gerou

Doretta's Song

(from *La rondine*)

Giacomo Puccini (1858–1924)
Arranged by Tom Gerou

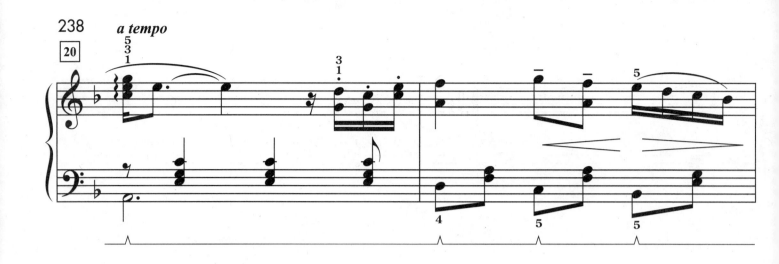

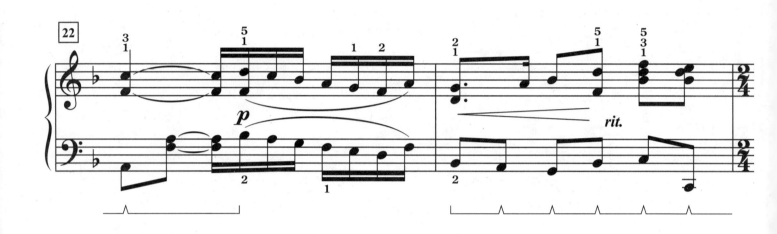

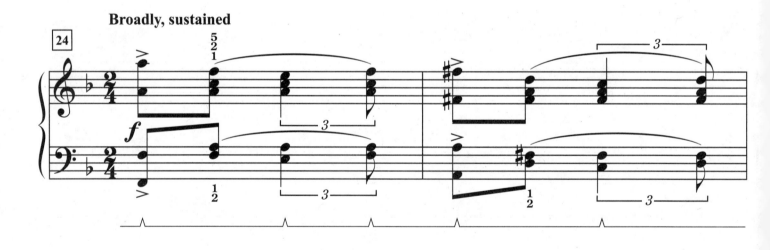

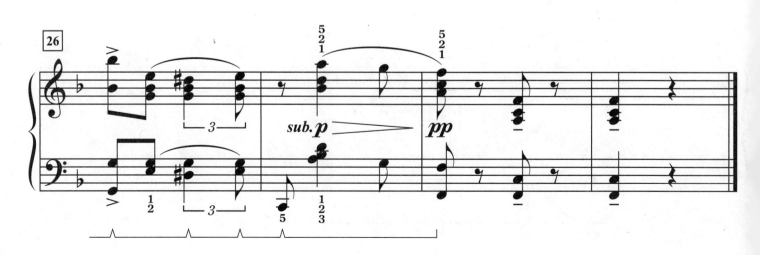

Un bel dì

(from *Madama Butterfly*)

Giacomo Puccini (1858–1924)
Arranged by Tom Gerou

Andante, molto calmo

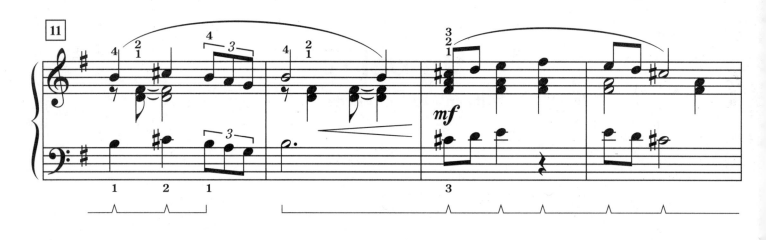

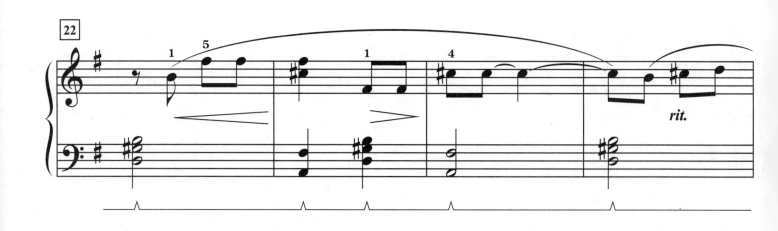

"Unfinished" Symphony

(Symphony No. 8, First Movement)

Franz Schubert (1797–1828)
D. 759
Arranged by Robert Schultz

Allegro moderato

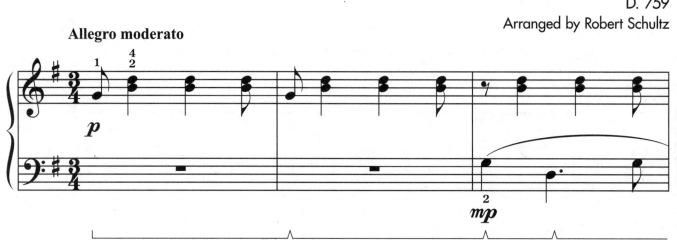

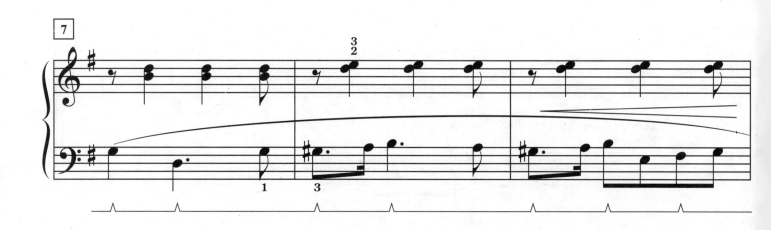

The Swan

(from *Carnival of the Animals*)

Camille Saint-Saëns (1835–1921)
Arranged by Carol Matz

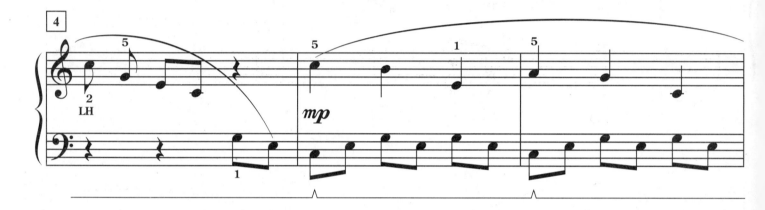

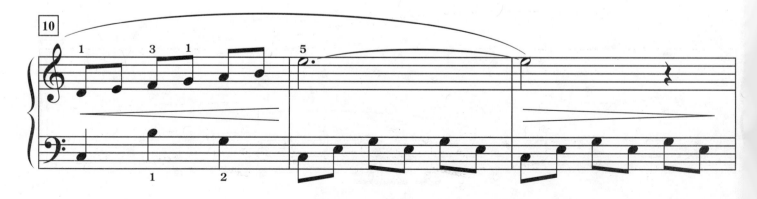

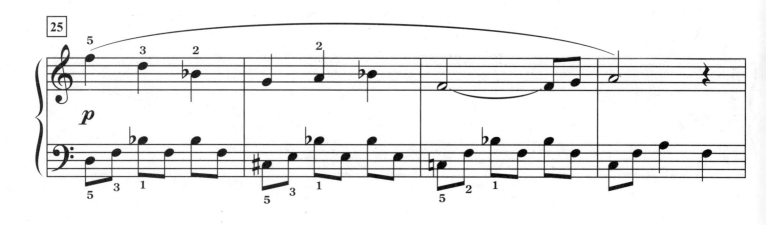

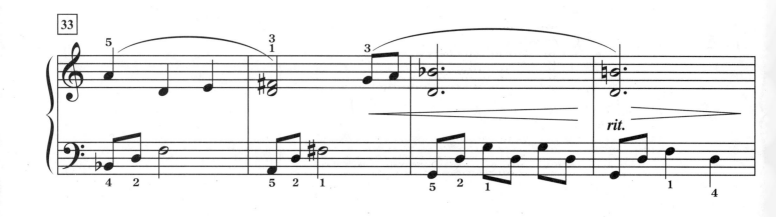

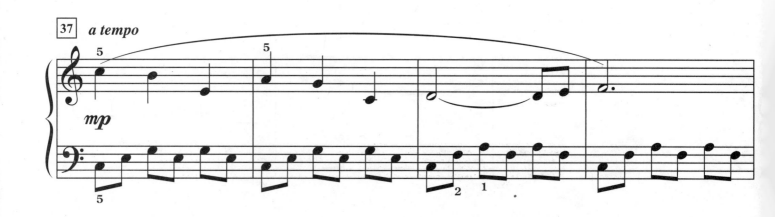

The Blue Danube

Johann Strauss, Jr. (1825–1899)
Op. 314
Arranged by Robert Schultz

Ständchen

Franz Schubert (1797–1828)
D. 957
Arranged by Carol Matz

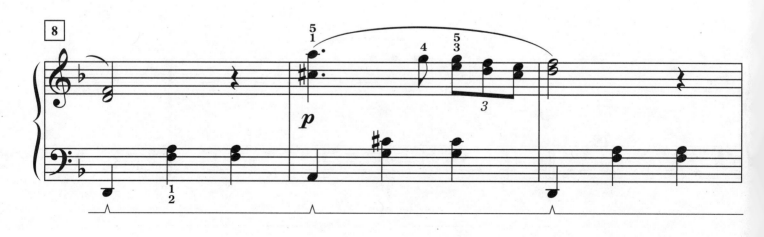

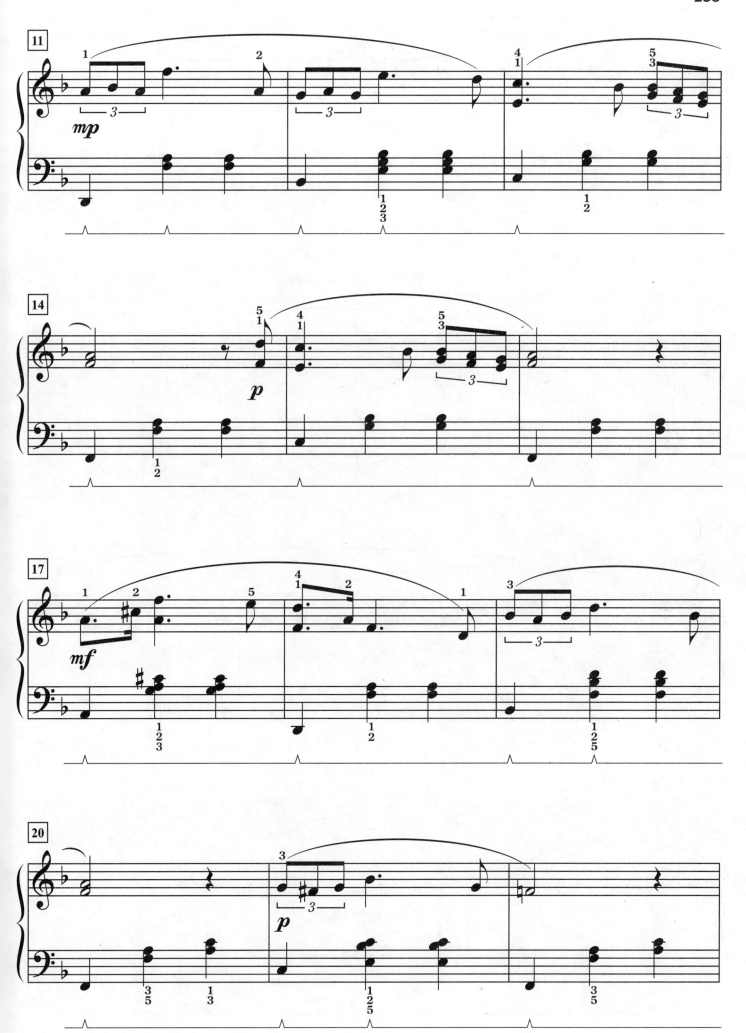

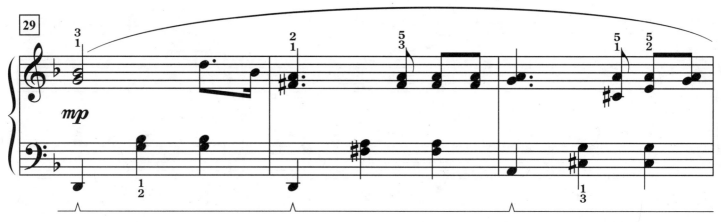

The Moldau (Vltava)

(from *Má vlast*)

Bedřich Smetana (1824–1884)
Arranged by Robert Schultz

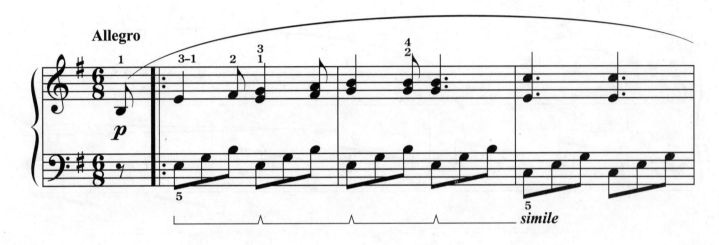

258

The Garland Waltz

(from *Sleeping Beauty*)

Peter Ilyich Tchaikovsky (1840–1893)
Op. 66
Arranged by Robert Schultz

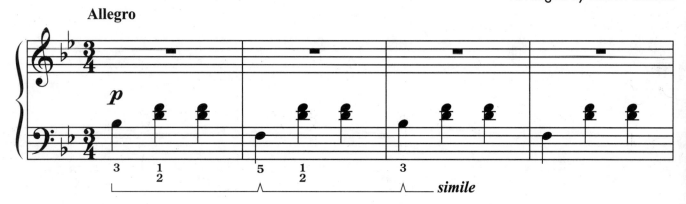

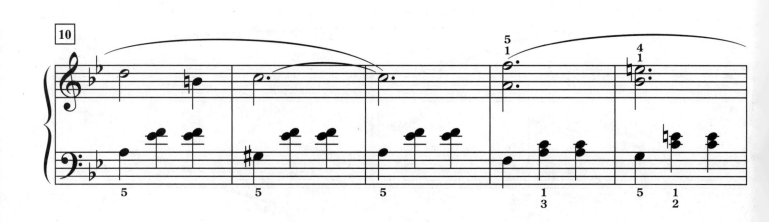

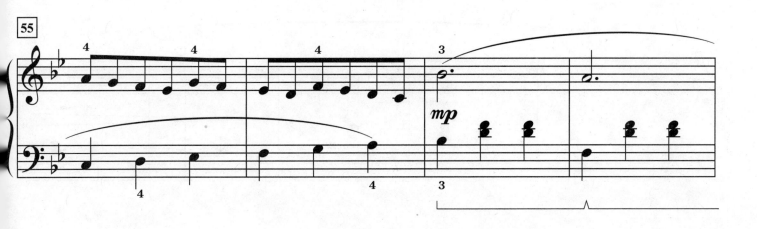

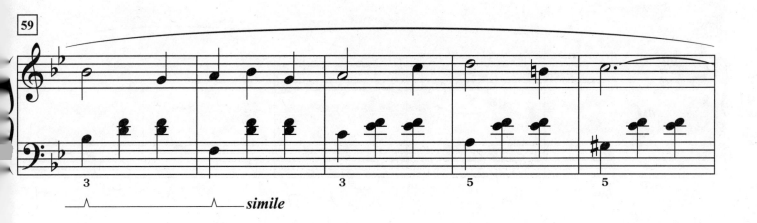

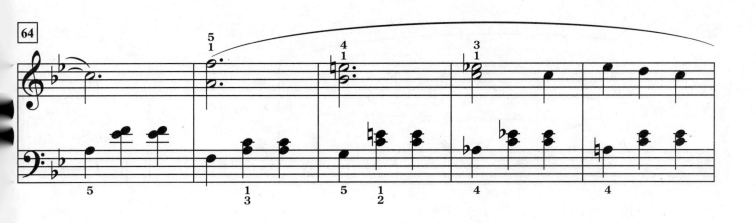

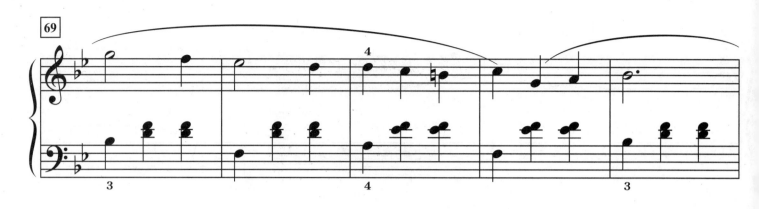

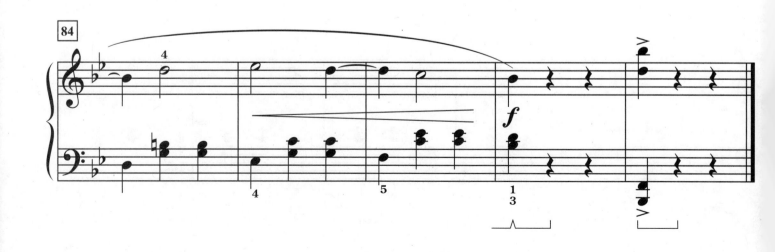

Piano Concerto No. 1

(First Movement)

Peter Ilyich Tchaikovsky (1840–1893)
Op. 23
Arranged by Carol Matz

Moderately

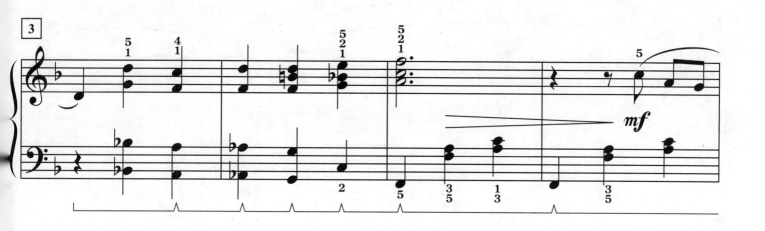

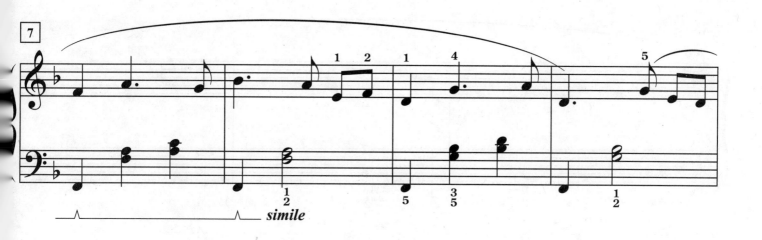

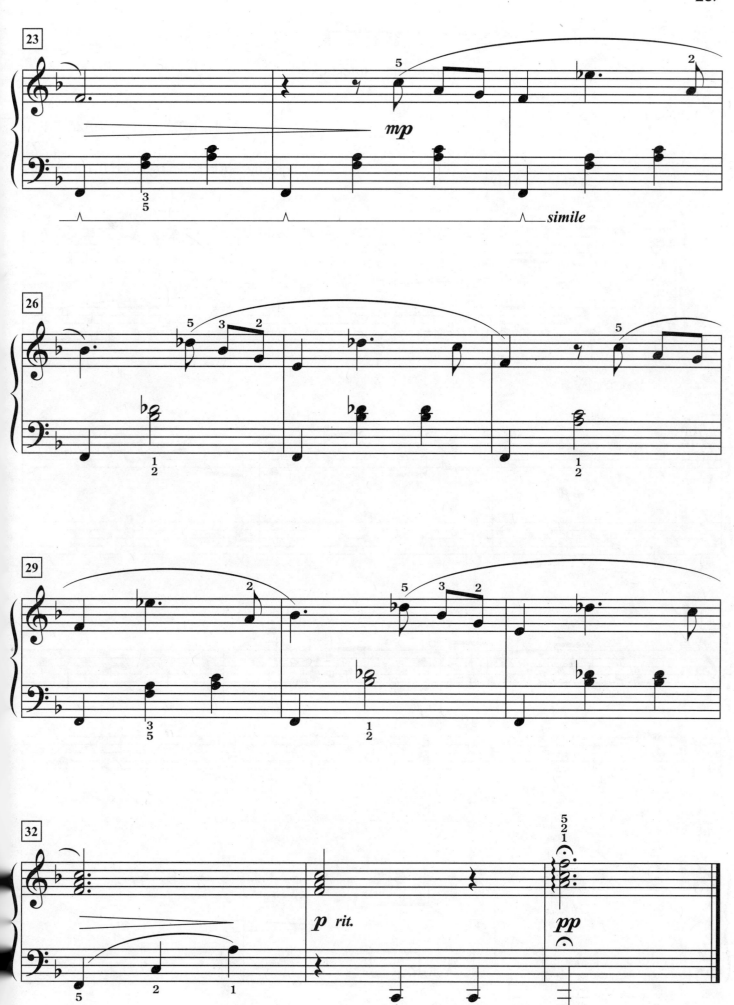

March

(from *The Nutcracker*)

Peter Ilyich Tchaikovsky (1840–1893)
Op. 71
Arranged by Gayle Kowalchyk and E. L. Lancaster

Tempo di marcia vivo

1812 Overture

Peter Ilyich Tchaikovsky (1840–14893)
Op. 49
Arranged by Carol Matz

Moderately fast

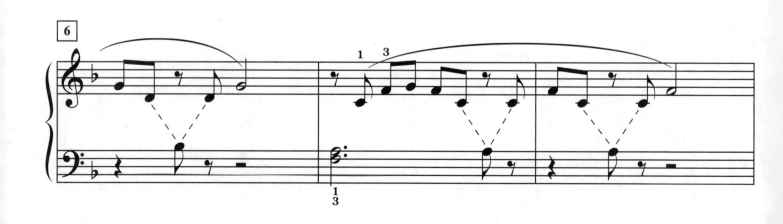

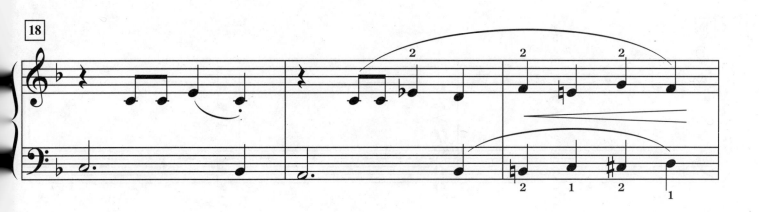

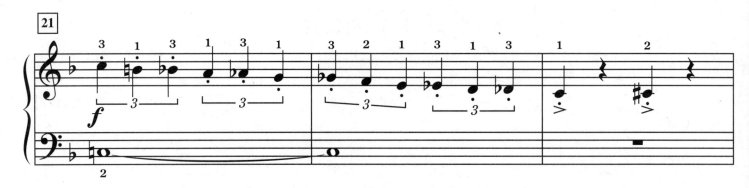

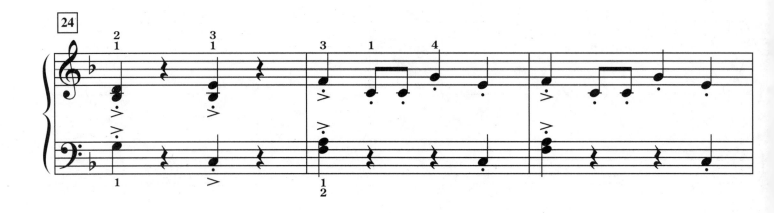

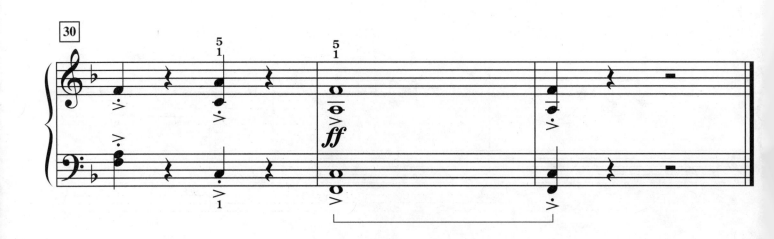

Act I Finale

(from *Swan Lake*)

Peter Ilyich Tchaikovsky (1840–1893)
Op. 20
Arranged by Carol Matz

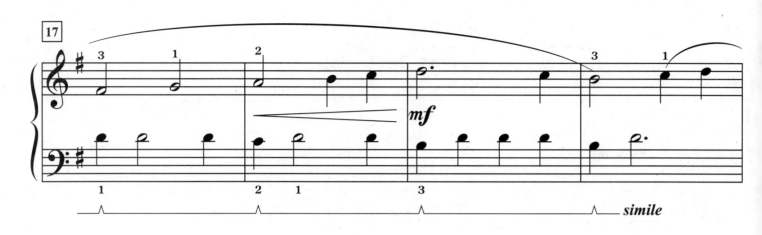

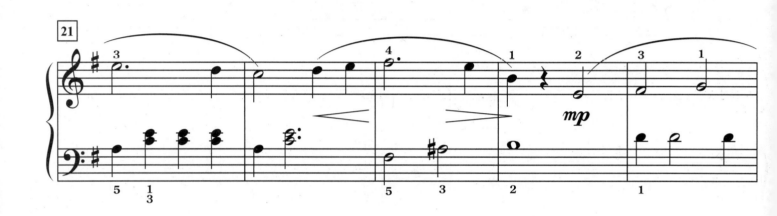

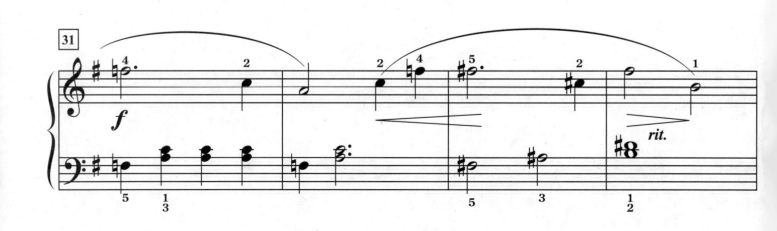

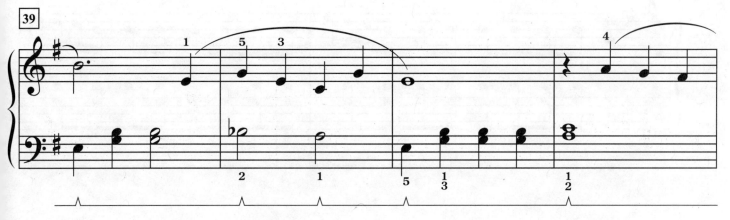

Anvil Chorus

(from *Il trovatore*)

Giuseppe Verdi (1813–1901)
Arranged by Tom Gerou

Allegro

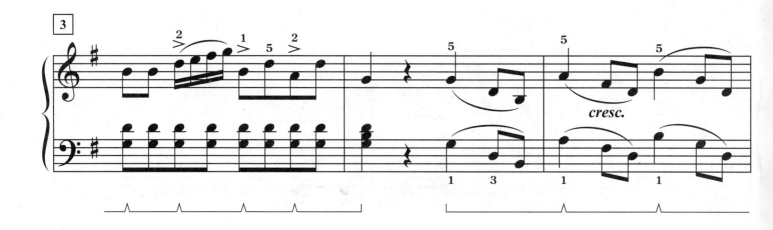

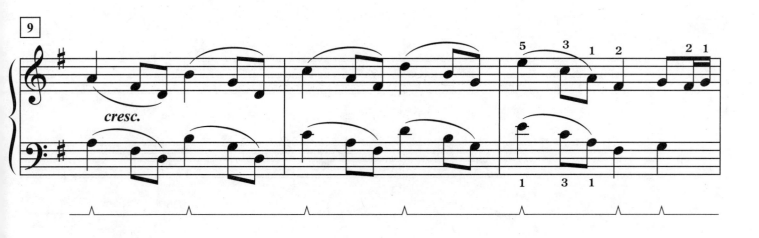

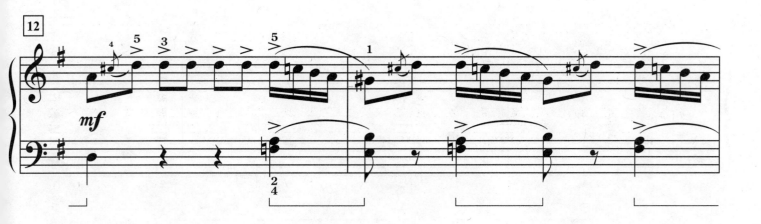

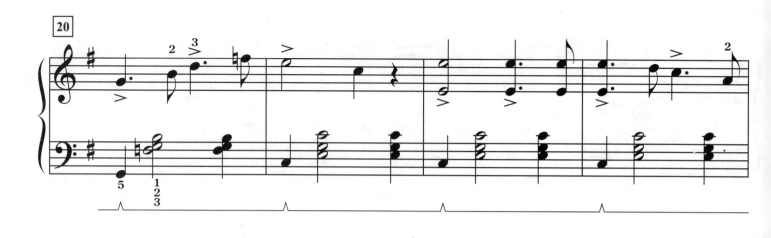

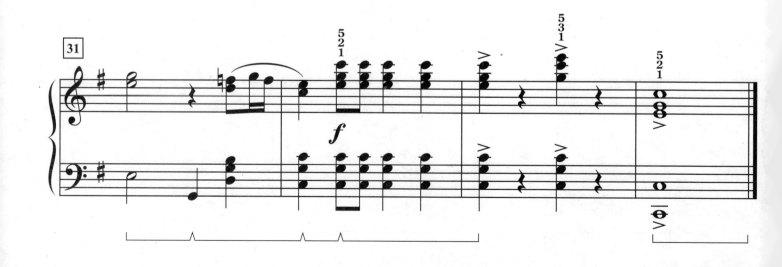

La donna è mobile

(from *Rigoletto*)

Giuseppe Verdi (1813–1901)
Arranged by Tom Gerou

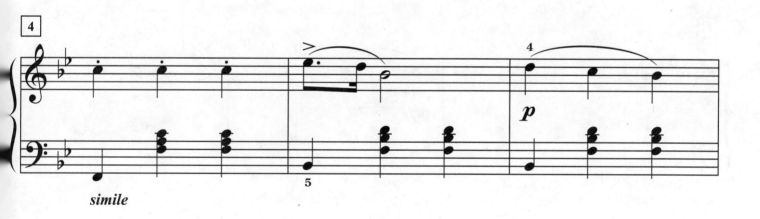

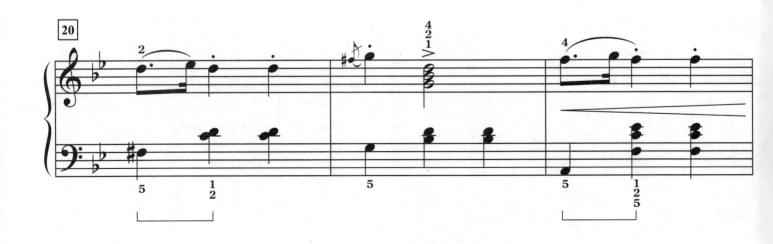

Libiamo

(from *La traviata*)

Giuseppe Verdi (1813–1901)
Arranged by Tom Gerou

Allegretto

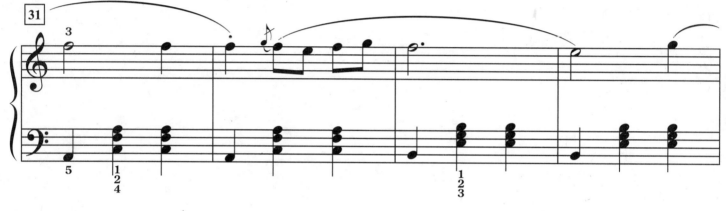

Bridal Chorus

(from *Lohengrin*)

Richard Wagner (1813–1883)
Arranged by Carol Matz

Mandolin Concerto in C Major

(First Movement)

Antonio Vivaldi (1678–1741)
RV 425
Arranged by Bruce Nelson

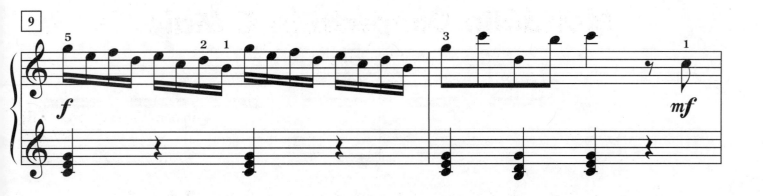

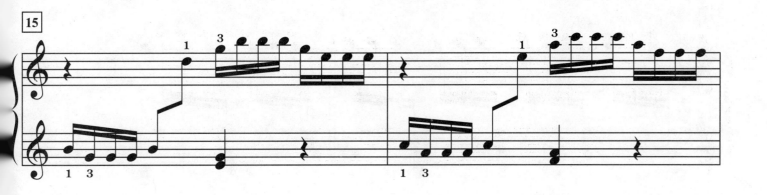

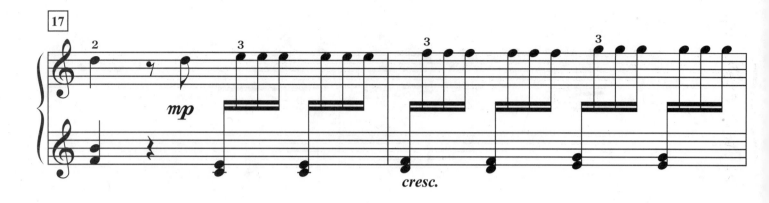

Spring

(from *The Four Seasons*)

Antonio Vivaldi (1678–1741)
Op. 8, No. 1, RV 269
Arranged by Bruce Nelson

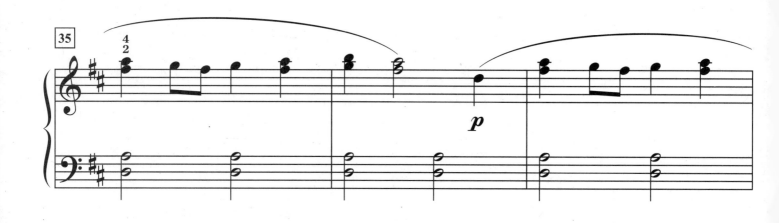